I'VE ONLY GOT TWO HANDS
AND I'M BUSY WRINGING THEM

I'VE ONLY GOT
TWO HANDS AND I'M
BUSY WRINGING

By Jane Goodsell   # THEM

Illustrated by Rob't Day

DOUBLEDAY & COMPANY, INC., GARDEN CITY, NEW YORK, 1966

Some of these chapters have appeared in a different form in *Good Housekeeping, Ladies Home Journal, American Weekly, Country Beautiful* and *Redbook.*

For Jim

CONTENTS

I'VE ONLY GOT TWO HANDS
AND I'M BUSY WRINGING THEM

ONE

MY FACE IS FAMILIAR, BUT . . .

My Face Is Familiar, But . . .

This book is not fiction. If I had the imagination to write a novel, I wouldn't make my central character a confused housewife who lives in a forty-two-year-old house with a leaky basement in Portland, Oregon. I'd invent a sixteen-year-old nymphomaniac who lives in Tangier, consorting with bull fighters, drug addicts and existentialist painters, and I'd write a passion-drenched saga of her search for identity.

But I lack the creativeness for that sort of thing. This

book is about *me* and my search for identity. It's not a memoir because My Story is weak on drama and suspense. I'm not an ex-spy or a reformed kleptomaniac or an erstwhile two-hundred-pound fatty who slimmed down to size ten. I *did* manage to kick the nail-biting habit when I was eleven, but I doubt if I could wring more than two or three inspirational chapters out of that struggle. I haven't performed any feats of heroism, either. I've never been marooned on a life raft nor parachuted from a burning plane. I gave birth to my three daughters in wedlock and under anesthesia, so I can't get much mileage out of that.

Okay. You've been warned about what this book *isn't*. But what *is* it? Well, as I said, it's about me. And who am I? That's the problem. I'm not quite sure.

The theme of this book was, I think, stated rather neatly by a police officer who waylaid me as I was proceeding against traffic up a one-way street. "Lady," he asked as he reached for his citation book, "just where do you think you're going?" The question, needless to say, was rhetorical. It was obvious to both of us that I hadn't the faintest notion.

Oh, certain vital statistics about me are clear enough. I have brown eyes, brown hair (slightly tinged with gray if I miss my appointment at the hairdresser's) and I stand five feet seven in my stocking feet.

I'm a wife. My husband has brown eyes and brown hair (always streaked with gray). He's four inches taller than I am, he edits a weekly newspaper and his name is Jim.

I'm the mother of three daughters: Ann, seventeen; Katie, fourteen; and Molly, seven and a half. Their eyes and hair are just the color you'd expect if you know anything about genes and chromosomes, but their behavior is less explicable. Certainly heredity doesn't account for Molly's fanatic fondness for animals (including little white mice with pink eyes who need a mommy to take care of them) or Katie's dreaminess. Katie can spend a whole Saturday morning not making her bed, while she thinks long thoughts about what she'd do with a million dollars or ponders what she'd be like if she were a boy. By contrast, Ann hasn't time to make her bed because she's busy composing lists. She catalogs her favorite records, books she intends to read, the colors of her hair ribbons and boys she's dated (listing them both chronologically and in descending order of preference).

I'm also a cook, a housekeeper, a registered voter, a chauffeur, a card-carrying member of the PTA and—well, I'm sure you get the picture. In short, I'm a fairly typical Modern American Woman. Come to think of it, I must be a pretty good subject to write about because other people have been doing it for years. They've analyzed me, pitied me, scolded me, cautioned me, advised me, cajoled me and snapped at me. Naturally, I'm flattered by all the attention, but I find it upsetting, too.

One afternoon I read an article purporting to be a lesson in love from Brigitte Bardot. The author accused me (the Modern American Woman) of being a steely, unfeminine, aggressive type who undermines her husband's masculinity and drives him to ulcers and heart attacks. The author urged me to buy myself a filmy peignoir and a bottle of seductive perfume, and to start behaving like a female.

But before I had time to put this new program into effect, I ran across another article titled "Women Are Moronic About Money." This author chastised me, the Modern American Woman, for being an empty-headed flutterbrain who hasn't the faintest understanding of economics. He scolded me for squandering money on frivolous luxuries (chiffon peignoirs?) and stated firmly that I should educate myself to discuss price-earnings ratios and corporate dividends with my husband.

You can see my predicament. What am I supposed to

do? Hustle into the peignoir, douse myself with Nuit d'Amour and curl up on my husband's lap for an interlude with the *Wall Street Journal?*

Now, I don't mind constructive criticism. (Well, that's not precisely true. I don't like any kind of criticism.) Still, I realize that I'm not perfect. I can use guidance and direction. I'm a born follower. But every time I plunge, full of zest and enthusiasm, into one area of self-improvement, along comes another critic, prodding me to tackle something else instead. Should I hearken to the message of *The Feminine Mystique* and seek fulfillment in work outside my home? Or should I follow the alternative advice, "Motherhood Is a Full-time Job"? Which diet should I go on? The Magic Hollywood Formula or the High Protein Reducing Plan? Or should I, instead, succumb to the siren song of the Food Editor who purrs, "Why Not Make Apple Strudel for Dinner Tonight"?

If my critics aren't telling me to stop doing something (Quit Worrying; Don't Nag Your Husband; Stop Pushing Your Children) they're urging me to start doing something: Knit Yourself a Coat; Investigate Your School's Dental Program; Raise Your Child's IQ; Try a New Short Hairdo; Plan Now for Your Husband's Retirement.

Possibly I could simplify my search for identity by giving up current literature and limiting my reading to the Harvard Classics. But I can't very well forswear shopping. And here again, in my role as a consumer, I'm mixed up. What sort of person do the manufacturers of America think I am? Do they consider me a fluffy little creature, a pampered darling, who's too fastidious to soil her fingertips with messy cream deodorants, too delicate to turn the handle of a nonelectric can opener? Or am I a sturdy, self-reliant amazon who's been eagerly awaiting the invention of the dripless paint roller which enables me to paint the living-room ceiling all by myself? My roll-on mascara (which takes the work out of my eye makeup chores) makes me feel cherished and protected. But the featherweight lawnmower (so light that even a woman can operate it) practically compels me to clamber into my dungarees and mow my own lawn. No wonder I can't find myself. I don't know who I'm looking for.

I know I ought to calm down, buck up and learn to adjust to life. But my reflexes aren't very fast, and I'm not as adjustable as all that. Take those magic-eye doors, for instance. My neighborhood supermarket installed them a few months ago. At first they unnerved me. I'd walk up to them, poised to push, and there wasn't anything to push. The doors popped open, and I nearly fell on my face. I finally made a successful adjustment. I got used to them. Now I expect all glass doors to open automatically. Sometimes they don't, which is hard on my nerves—not to mention my nose.

How about life doing a little adjusting to *me*? It seems symbolic that I'm in between sizes, too big for size twelve and too small for size fourteen. Nothing fits me. And my family is the wrong size. There are five of us, and recipes are calculated to serve four people or six. Since my grasp of fractions is rather weak, our refrigerator is always cluttered with little dabs of leftovers that nobody wants to eat. I suppose I ought to combine that half cup of spinach, the morsel of meat loaf, the single stuffed zucchini, the two wedges of cooked cabbage and that lone hot dog into a tasty casserole, topped with grated cheese. But even if I called it "Supper Delight," who'd eat it?

I don't want to give the impression that I'm dissatisfied with everything, and it worries me that this book may give the impression that I do nothing but complain. Nothing could be further from the truth. I am, in fact, the very model of patience and amiability. Oh, I won't pretend that it's easy keeping my composure. Life being as exasperating as it is, there are plenty of occasions when it seems positively negligent *not* to lose my temper and, if I could find somebody to get mad at, I'd scream. But who can I scream at?

My children? Certainly not. I've read all those articles warning that children's feelings of security depend on their mother being calm, understanding and emotionally stable. I can't yell at my husband either. I'm not even supposed to *nag* him (although I wish I knew how else to get him to trim the hedge) because well-adjusted adults are expected to resolve their problems through quiet, reasonable discussion. I'll confess that I don't exactly live up to this ideal. There have been occasions when I've lost control of myself and *raised my voice*. But my outbursts didn't have the therapeutic effect one might logically expect. I had barely cut loose before I was apologizing for losing my temper. I was, in fact, so overcome with remorse that I felt compelled to pay penance by baking homemade bread.

The knucklehead who ruined my skirt and sweater is a different problem altogether. I could shake him till his teeth rattled with no guilt pangs whatever. If I could get my hands on him, that is.

When I took my white sweater to the Busy Bee Cleaners & Dyers, I explained to the girl at the counter that I wanted it dyed to match my green skirt. She accepted it cheerfully and told me that it might not be possible to achieve the exact shade but it would be very close to it.

When I returned ten days later, the girl (a different girl this time) took my sweater and skirt off the rack and handed them to me, saying, "It's a perfect match, isn't it?" It was that, all right. Both the skirt and sweater were a bright, shocking *pink*. And so was I when I saw what had happened.

I was mad as hops. In an earlier, simpler age I'd have

swept past the counter and stormed into the back room, where I'd have sought out the knave who'd bungled the job. I'd have shaken my fist in his face and given him, in no uncertain language, a piece of my mind. Maybe he'd have apologized abjectly for his mistake. Maybe he'd have shrugged it off as "just one of those things that happen sometimes, lady." Maybe he'd have yelled at me for dumping a crazy, damfool dye job on him when he was so busy he didn't know if he was coming or going. Maybe he'd have called me names and threatened to dye *me* pink if I didn't go away and quit bothering him.

I don't know precisely what he'd have said, or what I'd have said, but at least *something* would have taken place. The episode would have had a climax.

The scene, as it was actually played, was far less dramatic. I couldn't storm into the back room because there wasn't any back room. The cleaning and dyeing plant was miles away on the outskirts of town. There was just that girl at the pickup-and-delivery branch, whose fault it certainly wasn't. It wouldn't be fair—or even fun—to scream and shake my fist at her.

In a cool, professional tone, she assured me that the matter would receive prompt attention and be resolved to my full satisfaction. I thanked her politely and left. What else could I do?

Two weeks later I got a check from Busy Bee, reimbursing me generously for my loss. There was a letter enclosed, apologizing for the mishap and expressing the hope that I would continue to give them my valued patronage. They couldn't have been nicer about the whole thing, but I still felt cheated. I'd been aced out of making a scene.

I can't blow my top at my congressman either. Not so's he'd notice it, anyway. I was incensed by a vote he cast, and I thought he ought to know how I felt. So I wrote him a letter to express my indignation. Since I wanted to impress him as an intelligent voter, I struggled over my syntax and pored through Bartlett's *Quotations* in search of apt literary allusions. By devoting two afternoons to the task, I composed a little masterpiece of caustic wit and biting irony; and I ended on a note of eloquence with a quotation from *Henry V.*

In retrospect, I think I should have skipped the rhetoric and spoken simply from the heart, saying, "Dear Mr. Congressman: Go soak your head."

Then he couldn't have answered me, "I am always happy to hear from my constituents, and I shall take your views under advisement." Then he couldn't have signed his letter, "Cordially yours . . ."

Or could he?

It's even more pointless to get mad at a little button. When I step into an elevator and push the "1" button to take me to the ground floor and, instead, find myself going up, up, up to the penthouse restaurant level, I'm irate. But what *at?*

This free-floating and undemonstrable indignation is, I think, symptomatic of contemporary life. And it's hard on the nervous system. Feeling exasperated, like falling in love, is miserable unless you can *do* something about it.

And that is why I wrote this book.

TWO

IF YOU CAN KEEP YOUR HEAD, HOW CAN YOU?

Quandaries I Quail In

Like poor Miniver Cheevy, I was born too late. I think I might have made a better adjustment in some bygone era when life was less complicated. The Stone Age? Too out-doorsy. The Renaissance? No, I couldn't live without my portable hair dryer. Contrariwise, there are a number of things I can't live *with* in this bedazzling century. I'm too indecisive, too namby-pamby to make the decisions that face me in this complex world.

I'm not talking about the farm surplus or the admission

of Red China to the United Nations. What bewilders me is peanut butter. I can't make up my mind whether to buy chunky style or creamy style. The creamy type is nice because it's so smooth and—well, creamy. But on the other hand, the chunky style has a good, crunchy texture, so maybe . . . no, on second thought, perhaps the creamy style is better after all, but still . . .

I'd forget the whole thing and buy honey instead, but then I'd have to decide between the jar, the carton, the comb and the squeeze bottle.

I'm puzzled about bobby pins, too. I don't know whether to buy the straight-edged or crinkly-edged type. There must be *some* reason why I should prefer one or the other. But why? And which?

Worst of all are those lovely decorator colors. Everything from ballpoint pens to dustpans comes in eight assorted shades to suit my personality. But I don't *have* as much personality as all that. I like each and every one of those pretty colors. I'm scared that someday I'll go to pieces right in the middle of the supermarket. I'll be standing at the paper products counter, trying to decide between aqua- and peach-colored roller towels, and suddenly something inside me will snap, and I'll throw myself on the floor and sob.

Talking about colors reminds me, not surprisingly, of talking about colors, which I can't do—not any more. Those modern decorator shades have such esoteric names that I can't discuss them with any degree of confidence because I'm not sure which is which. I don't know periwinkle from cobalt or burnt almond from coffee bean. I'm not color-blind. I know green when I see it, but the trouble is, I don't see it. What I consider green turns out to be pistachio or loden or lime or mint. Once there was a color called brown. Now they call it chutney or tobacco or *café au lait*.

They do. I don't. I still call it brown. I try not to, but I can't help it.

Just the other day a friend told me she was doing over her living room in shades of curry and moss with touches of pomegranate, and did I think her citrus chair would blend with her decorating scheme? I stood there, blinking, as I tried to translate what she'd said into meaningful terms. Finally I blurted, "Oh, you mean your *yellow* chair!"

She gazed at me with ill-concealed contempt, and that was the last I heard of her decorating problems.

Colors called hyacinth and nasturtium don't give me any mental image at all. Cornflower poses a different problem. I do get an image, but the wrong one. To me, cornflower sounds yellow, but it's really blue. And cerise, which makes me see yellow, is bright pink. I can translate pewter into gray (although it takes me a while) but mushroom eludes me, and I confuse persimmons with kumquats.

Not so long ago I ran into a poignant situation over eggplant. With a birthday check in hand, I walked into one of those dress shops so austerely elegant that no clothes are visible. They discuss a dress with you before they let you see it. The saleslady described a little chiffon after-five frock with a crushed neckline and a graceful skirt in a lovely eggplant shade. I asked if I might see it, but when she brought it out I gasped, "Purple! Oh, I can't wear purple!"

The saleslady's eyebrows shot up to her hairline. "I *told* you it was eggplant," she said reprovingly.

I turned red—I mean, cerise—with embarrassment. My mistake was, I was thinking of *cooked* eggplant.

I've got problems with my electric blanket, too. I can't decide where to set the dial. Position 6 seems comfortable enough, neither too hot nor too cold but just right. Or is it? Mightn't 7 be just a teensy bit cozier? Or maybe 5 would be preferable for all-night sleeping comfort. Perhaps

I should spin the dial like a roulette wheel, and leave the decision up to chance.

Some nights, as I lie awake fiddling with the heat control, it seems to me I had an easier time back in the old days when I faced only two disagreeable choices: (1) I could curl up in a ball and try to forget that I was cold; or (2) I could drag myself out of bed, and rummage around the house for an extra blanket.

Life was simple and primitive in those days. Stockings didn't come in proportioned sizes and washing machine dials had two settings: ON and OFF. Ironing boards weren't adjustable, telephones were black and pillowslips were white, and face powder wasn't blended to match the underlying radiance of true skin tones. You could count the varieties of breakfast cereal on your fingers, and the

different types of rice on your thumbs. Six delicious flavors
were a many-splendored variety.

It was a world of limited choices. Oh, it had its draw-
backs, no doubt about that. I remember how I used to
grumble that my ironing board was too low, and my
stockings bagged at the ankles. My face powder was a
different color than I was, and my telephone clashed
with my decor. But my psyche was in better shape than it
is today. This color-coordinated, proportionately sized, fin-
gertip-adjustable, multiple-choice world is too much for
the likes of me.

Buying a lipstick requires more soul searching than choosing a husband. First I must decide among a dozen brands,
each promising to make me glamorous, seductive and ir-
resistible. Then I must make up my mind whether I want
my lips to have a satiny sheen or a lustrous luminescence.
And finally I must decide which of twenty-two radiantly
flattering shades was created just for me.

Buying a package of cigarettes is no simple matter of
asking for a pack of Marmadukes, please. The way they
fire questions at me, I feel as though I'm being cross-exam-
ined on the witness stand. Long or short? Filtered or
regular? Cork-tipped or plain? Fliptop box or soft-pack? I
stammer, gulp and shuffle my feet, and finally become so
confused that I end up buying a brand I've always dis-
liked.

I'm aware, of course, that everyone isn't like me. Some
people have lightning reflexes and firm convictions, even
when faced with a dizzying array of choices. I know there
are people like that because I saw one of them in action.
I was leaning against a bakery counter, my chin propped
on my hands, as I stared at the loaves of bread on the
shelves. I was trying to decide whether I wanted potato
bread, buttercrust, egg twist (topped with poppy seeds,
sesame seeds or plain), sourdough French, hearth-baked

French, Vienna bread, oatmeal bread, pumpernickel, orange-nut or cinnamon, and whether I wanted it in a small loaf or large, unsliced, thin-sliced or regular.

As the salesclerk drummed her fingers on the counter and I stood there biting my lip, this woman marched in. She swept a glance over the loaves on the shelves and calmly announced that she wanted a small loaf of egg twist with poppy seeds, unsliced.

Now *there's* a woman who is master of her fate and captain of her soul. I'll bet *she* has no trouble deciding whether to set her alarm clock to Loud or Soft. I'll bet she can walk into a hosiery department and state precisely the denier, gauge, toe style, seam specification, shade and proportioned size that she wants. I wouldn't even be surprised if she could read through a menu offering forty kinds of hamburger sandwiches and unhesitatingly order a pizzaburger.

As for me, it's a critical moment when I have to decide whether to wear my reversible raincoat with the plaid side in or out.

I know I ought to be a child of my century—brisk, decisive and firm. But I'm not built that way. When I was in grade school, I used to squirm with indecision every time I had to decide between chocolate, vanilla and strawberry. Today, with every ice cream shop featuring twenty-six flavors, I'm beside myself. I try to keep calm. I steel myself with vows that *this* time I will make my choice in a cool, adult, authoritative manner, that I won't panic. But it seems that every time—well, what happened last week is a good example. I walked into an ice cream shop, bristling with determination. I wouldn't even look at the flavor chart to see what Today's Special might be. I would simply ask for a quart of vanilla.

And that's what I did. I asked for a quart of vanilla.

The counter girl clicked to attention. "Plain or French vanilla?" she asked.

"Uh—plain," I said.

"Regular or low-calorie?"

"Regular."

"Soft or hard frozen?"

I clenched my fists. "Soft. No, I mean hard!"

"Brick or hand-packed?"

And that's when I went out of focus. I walked over to the ice cream freezer and reached into it.

Grabbing a carton, I bleated, "I'll take this!"

And that's how I happened to buy licorice ripple.

Newspapers upset me, too, because I can't seem to grasp what I read. It isn't the words that puzzle me, although I'll confess that I'm not sure where Tanzania is, and I can't pronounce Dongxoai. What really defeats me, though, are the numbers. For example, I read that the output of men's undershorts was 2,328,000 dozen for the quarter year. Now think about this for a minute. I mean, *really* think about it. Can you wrap your mind around all those undershorts? And don't forget they're talking about dozens, not pairs. To get a true picture, you'd have to multiply 2,328,000 by 12—a clearly impossible task.

Can anyone grasp the eye-bugging figures that newspapers toss off with airy nonchalance? Do you, for example, comprehend how many dollars it takes to make $1.8 billion? Can you picture 1,689,745 candy bars in your mind's eye? When you stop to think about it, does the figure 1,000,000 mean anything except six zeros? Not to me, it doesn't. Exactly how much *is* a million anyway? Let's stop to think about it.

The number 100 seems a sensible starting point. I understand the concept of 100 as clearly as Euclid because I once made 100 meatballs for a potluck supper. It took me all day, and I used every mixing bowl in the kitchen. When the meatballs were finished, they filled my large preserving kettle to the brim. One hundred is an awful lot of meatballs.

Now, 1,000 meatballs would fill 10 kettles. And 100 kettles would hold—I'm working with paper and pencil now—why, 100 kettles would hold only 10,000 meatballs! We're nowhere near a million, and I can't bear the thought of any more meatballs. They're so greasy. There must be a faster, neater way to reach 1,000,000.

Is it possible that I've made a million beds? It wouldn't surprise me. Let's assume that I've made five beds a day, every day, for the past nineteen years. (Now that I think about it, I haven't made five beds a day because I didn't start marriage with three children, but let's not quibble over details.) Okay. We'll multiply five beds a day by 365 days a year. That makes 1,825 beds I make each year. Now we'll multiply 1,825 by nineteen years, and we get . . . 34,675. I *think* that's correct. Anyway, it's a lot of bedmaking, but it's a long, long way from a million.

I give up. My imagination is too limited to comprehend a million of anything. Besides, now that we've entered the space age, it's probably pointless to worry about a commonplace number like 1,000,000. We're slopping around in billions and trillions, and I just don't believe that anyone—not even a mathematician—can grasp that many zeros. Isn't that why we have computers?

Time is another conundrum. It, too, baffles me, but I must somehow come to grips with it. The problem isn't Daylight Saving Time. I can understand that, sort of. What I can't master is Modern Indefinite Time, the guessing game of figuring out when to keep an appointment. For instance:

What time should I get to a ten o'clock meeting?
I hate to admit it, but I used to be so naïve that I'd

arrive at ten sharp, leaving the dishes in the sink and the beds unmade. I was in such a hurry to get there on time that I'd forget my gloves and speed across town, skimming through yellow lights and hoping my watch was fast. On arrival, I'd dash into the meeting hall to find nobody there but the building custodian, who'd be setting up the folding chairs, and the chairman of the refreshment committee, who'd ask me to be an angel and make the coffee for her.

Little by little I broke the punctuality habit. I began by arriving five minutes late and gradually built up to forty. Give or take a few minutes, twenty to eleven seemed a sensible time to arrive for a ten o'clock meeting. But Modern Indefinite Time is shifty by its very nature. A few weeks ago I arrived at a meeting barely thirty minutes late and—would you believe it?—they'd already whipped through the Minutes of the Last Meeting, dispensed with Old and New Business and elected *me* chairman of the White Elephant Sale!

What time should I expect the plumber who promised to show up first thing in the morning?

Of course, I don't actually expect him to appear at eight o'clock sharp but, on the other hand, can I count on him *not* to? There seems to be an unfortunate cause-and-effect relationship operating here. If I assume that he won't arrive before ten, he'll bang on the door at 8:02 and have the pipes turned off before I've had time to draw water for coffee. But if I take him at his word (and get up half an hour early and rush everyone through breakfast because the plumber is due) he won't show up until three days later. At two in the afternoon, just as I'm lathering my hair with a copper-glow rinse that's supposed to be washed out in twenty minutes.

Incidentally, how long is a jiffy? It's one hour and fifteen minutes according to the last plumber who assured me that he'd turn the water back on in a jiffy.

What time should I arrive for a one o'clock lunch date with a friend?

It depends on (a) how late I think she'll be, which depends on (b) how late she thinks I'll be.

The point is, I want to arrive later than my friend, so that I can rush in, full of breathless explanations about my hectically busy morning. But she, too, has a reputation to maintain as a vibrant young matron whose life buzzes with activities. So how late is late enough?

If I arrive at 1:20 and she doesn't get there until 1:40, I will, of course, insist that I arrived just a second ago myself; and I'll spend the whole lunch trying to convince her that my life is busier and more frantic than anybody's.

But next time I've simply *got* to be the last to arrive, even if it means spending a whole hour combing my hair in the powder room.

What time should I keep a 10:30 appointment with the doctor?

I know the answer to this question: Eleven o'clock at the earliest. Nevertheless, I get there at 10:30 sharp because I foresee what would happen if I didn't. It would turn out to be the one day, unique in a lifetime of medical practice, when the doctor was keeping his appointments on time.

I wouldn't dream of keeping the doctor waiting. Like all Dr. Casey fans, I realize that the doctor's time is more valuable than mine. I know this but, after a forty-minute wait in the reception room during which not a single patient is ushered in, I can't help wondering. What is that man doing in there anyway? Working a crossword puzzle? Playing solitaire? Talking to his broker? And there I sit, when I could be home catching up on the ironing.

If I've arranged to pick up my husband in front of his office building at 5:30, what time should I get there?

In this situation, I have my pick of two choices: (1) I

can get there at 5:30, and drive round and round the block in rush hour traffic, getting madder by the minute, until my husband shows up; or (2) I can get there at 5:45, leaving him standing on a street corner, getting madder by the minute, until I show up.

Theoretically—since he's late half the time, and I'm late half the time—we should occasionally arrive simultaneously. This has happened. Back in the spring of '61, as I recall.

What time should I show up for a seven o'clock dinner party?

Of all situations involved in Modern Indefinite Time, this is the most hazardous. It's the hardest to guess right, and the worst when you guess wrong. The ideal time to ring the doorbell is *after* the early arrivals have been served the first round of drinks and the conversation has revved up a bit, but *before* the canapés have begun to wilt. Try as I do, I find this an unattainable goal. The problem is not *whether* to be late, but *how* late.

Basically, guessing right is an intuitive thing. But sometimes, if you listen closely, you can extract a clue from the phrasing of the invitation. If your hostess says, "Come about seven," you needn't draw your bath until 6:45. If she says, "Sevenish," you can give yourself a manicure, too, and take plenty of time for the polish to dry. If she simply says "Come at seven," maybe you ought to get there by 7:30.

And then again, maybe not. As an extra precaution, I always take a reading on the parking situation around the house when we arrive. If we can park within half a block, I urge my husband to drive around for a while.

One night, as we were making our fourth turn around the block, Jim remarked that there seemed to be a lot of traffic for that time of night in a residential district. In fact, we seemed to be in some sort of procession. As it turned out, three other couples, who were as reluctant as we to be the first to arrive, were making the rounds with us. When we pulled up in front of the house, they followed suit. We all arrived in a bunch, an hour late.

The dinner, like all dinners adjusted to Modern Indefinite Time, survived beautifully. It was a carefree casserole with an exotic name—scampeloni or tortella or something like that. At least I *guess* it survived beautifully. I've no idea what it was supposed to taste like.

But the hostess looked a bit drawn, and the host looked sort of squinty-eyed, and the martini pitcher was half empty.

What time should we arrive for 6:30 dinner at my great-aunt Hattie's house?

Aunt Hattie is hopelessly out of step with the times. She's a martinet about punctuality. When you go to her house for dinner, you eat rare roast beef and Yorkshire pudding and asparagus with hollandaise sauce, and you're expected to show up at 6:30. Six thirty-five at the very latest.

Aunt Hattie is a fixed point in a bewildering universe, and I love to be invited to her house. It's so relaxing to know what's expected of me.

I Love Him, But . . .

I fixed his favorite dinner. Pot roast and potato pancakes, glazed carrots, tossed salad with croutons and, for dessert, homemade apple pie.

Weary but proud, I placed it on the table and called my husband to dinner.

"Oh, I forgot to tell you," he said, "I've decided to take off a few pounds."

He bought himself a guitar a few years ago, but he's never learned to play it. He has an expensive camera with a light meter, a range finder and a close-up attachment, but he hasn't figured out how to work it. He has a basement full of tools, including six different kinds of saws, but he hired a carpenter to build a little shelf for the back porch.

One day, while he was rummaging for a bottle opener in a kitchen drawer, he picked up my twenty-nine-cent melon ball cutter and asked, "What's this?"

I explained what it was, and he said, "Do you ever use it?"

I confessed that I didn't because—well, it was easier not to.

He said, "Then what did you buy it for?"

He uses my manicure scissors to cut rope and my eyebrow tweezers for tying trout flies. He bathed the dog with my oatmeal complexion soap. He used up all my dustcloths for kite tails.

But if he catches me using his razor or borrowing his third-best sweatshirt (the one with the sleeves cut off and the broken zipper) he stares at me in astonishment.

"That," he says, "is mine."

Molly, our seven-year-old, awoke at 3 A.M. with a fever of 102.5. I dumped her into a tub of lukewarm water, gave her five grains of aspirin and tucked her back into bed, while my husband chain-smoked and muttered about phoning the doctor.

I explained that little children get higher fevers than adults and, anyway, she seemed to be better now. When he reached the stage of smoking two cigarettes at the same time, I said, "All right, go ahead and call the doctor. You won't be able to sleep unless you do."

So he telephoned the doctor and said, "I hate to call at this hour, but our little girl has a high temperature, and my wife is terribly worried about her."

I was determined to tell a joke right for once. I rehearsed it to a fine polish before I said to him: "Have you heard the story about the young man who took the night train from Florence to Zurich? As he was walking down the aisle, he bumped into a beautiful girl and he said, 'Pardon me, miss, but—'"
"Yep," said my husband. "Good joke, isn't it?"

I yearned for a striped cashmere sweater for my birthday, but I didn't want to come right out and ask for it because it's much more fun to be surprised. So I dropped hints like a bridesmaid scattering rice. I mentioned the amazing coincidence that my age and my sweater size would be exactly the same on my birthday. I clipped a newspaper advertisement, marked it with red pencil and left it lying by the telephone for three days. On my birthday he gave me a book he'd been wanting to read and a check because, he explained, he had no way of knowing what I wanted.

"I had a terrific bridge hand this afternoon," I said as I dished up the peas at dinner. "The ace, king and three little spades; the ace, jack of diamonds; a singleton king of clubs, and four hearts to the ace, queen, jack. I bid two spades, my partner said two no trump, south bid three clubs and I closed at four spades."
"What did you jump for?" asked my husband. "If you'd bid three hearts, you could have gotten some more information from your partner."
"But I made it!" I cried triumphantly. "Four spades, doubled and redoubled!"

"Pure luck," said my husband. "But next time don't make the mistake of . . ."

He talks eloquently about the barbarism of large cocktail parties. He says the food is terrible, it's impossible to talk and there's no place to sit down. Being a loyal wife (and lacking anything new to wear) I turned down a cocktail party invitation, explaining that we had a previous engagement.

When I told my husband of the sacrifice I'd made for his sake, he looked shocked and said, "Whatever gave you the idea I wouldn't want to go?"

I bought eight dollars' worth of eye makeup, and I spent an hour in the bathroom, experimenting until I achieved just the effect I wanted—a doe-eyed look with a dash of sparkle. I sought out my husband, who was in the den, waiting for me to go to a dinner party. I stood before him, batting my eyelashes.

"Well," I said, "how do you like it?"

He looked at me for a long time and then he said, "Ummmm, very nice. That's a good color on you. Turn around and let me see the back. I think maybe the whatchamacallit—the hem—is a little too short."

When I reach the absolute end of my rope, turn purple and scream that he's the most difficult, contradictory and impossible man in the whole wide world, he puts his hand under my chin, kisses me on the end of my nose and says, "I *like* a woman with spirit. Did you know that your eyes turn green when you get mad?"

And that's the most infuriating thing of all. I can't stay mad at him.

Frailty, Thy Name Is Who?

Back in the days when women were The Weaker Sex, a lady could take to her bed with a case of the vapors and recline there in dignity and comfort. No apologies were made, no questions asked. Whatever the vapors were (my guess is that they were just an old-fashioned version of jangled nerves) they constituted a respectable excuse for staying in bed.

Today the vapors are as outmoded as smelling salts and there is—alas!—little hope of their coming back into vogue.

Today's cure for the heebie-jeebies is a tranquilizing tablet. This is progress? Not to me, it isn't. I don't want fast, fast, fast relief. I want to recover slowly—in bed.

Modern science has knocked the heart out of the time-honored institution of staying-in-bed. About the only excuses left are (1) surgery, (2) childbirth and (3) fevers over 102 degrees. And even these have been nibbled at by that old spoilsport, science. By the time you're feeling well enough to enjoy being in bed, you're cured, up and back in the kitchen stirring oatmeal.

In case you haven't noticed, I'm talking about women. None of what I've said applies to men, who have no difficulty at all taking to their beds with clear consciences— now that they are firmly established as The Weaker Sex.

Men know for a fact that their wives will outlive them by a good six years. Don't all the statistics say so? Or take those newspaper accounts of people dropping dead in the streets. Any man can tell you that all the victims are male. Things like that make a man stop and think. And think and think and think. They also give his wife pause. After all, she doesn't want to be a widow. The result is that women worry about men, and men worry about themselves.

Men view health as an all-or-nothing situation. If they're not feeling tiptop, they're sick. And if they're sick, it's serious. They refuse to settle for anything but the worst. To the best of my knowledge, there has never been an authenticated case of male sniffles.

When a man stumbles home from work in the middle of the day, pointing to his throat and gasping, "Honey, I'm sick!" he means he's *sick*. In quavering voice, he lists his symptoms: his ears are ringing; his head throbbing; he has a curious numb sensation in his left knee; his tongue is coated.

Obviously his condition is critical. Get him to bed! Call

the doctor! Bring him hot-water bottles and cold poultices! Rub his back and murmur, "Poor darling."

Now, I'm not intimating that the sufferings of ailing males aren't real and terrible. Quite the contrary. A man with a touch of indigestion, complicated by an attack of male mortality statistics, leading him to suspect that he is beyond medical aid and it's only a matter of time, is indeed a poor darling; and only the most callous, hardhearted wife could fail to respond to his panic.

Still, it's worth mentioning that those scary statistics, which incontestably prove his frailty, have enabled him to perform a feat that is next to impossible for a woman. He is spending the day in bed.

I wouldn't dream of suggesting that women emulate men by becoming hypochondriacs themselves. Women couldn't play the role with any real conviction, now that science has proved them virtually indestructible. Anyway, women lack the dramatic flair for that sort of thing. They're more stolid and less imaginative than men, which is probably a good thing. No marriage could withstand the hysteria that would result if women were as sensitive and excitable as their husbands.

Even so, women aren't all *that* calm and placid, and being members of The Stronger Sex is something of a strain. Our sudden elevation to physical superiority was, in itself, a shock. We had previously considered ourselves fragile, flowerlike creatures and it jolted us to learn that, as science puts it, "women are physically tougher than men because their extra fatty layer gives them additional natural protection." (Wouldn't you think they could find a happier way to phrase it?)

Be that as it may, women met the challenge with characteristic fortitude. They began shouldering burdens that were formerly considered the rightful province of the man-of-the-house. To spare their husbands the nervous stress of paying the monthly bills, women assumed the task of balancing the checkbook. Gone were the days when a lady could kittenishly wheedle her husband to buy her a fur coat or a new living-room carpet. Now she knew only too well that they couldn't afford such extravagance. Worse yet, she had to convince *him* that they couldn't swing the new convertible he'd set his heart on—or the rod and reel which, unbeknownst to her, he'd bought already.

To save their husbands from overexerting themselves, women quit saying, "Just wait till your father gets home!" and scolded the kids themselves. It no longer seemed fair to saddle men with the entire job of running the world, so women pitched in to help. They organized boards and committees. They spearheaded civic reforms. They joined the League of Women Voters so they could assist their husbands in marking the ballot.

To provide an atmosphere of relaxed serenity in the home, they learned how to mix martinis so they could have a tinkling pitcher waiting when Father straggled in from the office; and to prove that they were good sports (not to mention the fact that they, too, needed resuscitation by 6 P.M.) they joined him in a cocktail.

Being justifiably worried about their husbands' susceptibilities, they developed a protective attitude and urged their menfolk to take better care of themselves: to cut down on their smoking, to get more exercise, to bundle up in bad weather, to skip the second helping and the third highball.

Instead of being grateful for all this help and solicitude, men felt uneasy. They chided women for being aggressive, bossy and unfeminine. They complained that women were domineering . . . trying to run things . . . usurping male prerogatives and chipping away at male masculinity.

And women, whose most basic desire is to please men, began searching their souls and asking themselves if maybe men weren't right. Perhaps women *were* losing their femininity. In actual fact, it mattered very little if men were right or wrong in feeling as they did. The point was that they *felt* that way. And if men didn't like the way women were behaving, women would simply have to act differently. But *how?* Having been irrevocably proved the hardier sex, women could scarcely go back to swooning and needlepoint. In light of the new scientific evidence that would not only be silly but downright immoral. They would be shirking their responsibilities.

Gradually the rules were redefined and a new concept in femininity evolved. The archetype of modern womanhood—created by a coalition of social scientists, editors, psychologists and public opinion pollsters—emerged on the scene.

She is competent, vigorous, astute, athletic, indomitable —but *feminine*. She is expected to do everything men do, but in a graceful, charming, ladylike way. And on top of all that, she must be a creative cook, a patient and understanding mother, a gracious hostess and a radiant beauty. In short, the modern woman is supposed to be a composite of Lyndon Johnson, Audrey Hepburn and Marmee in *Little Women*.

No matter how sturdy a sex you belong to, that's quite an assignment. I won't say it's impossible. Meeting the challenge successfully may provide a lady with such a sense of accomplishment that she can keep going on sheer exaltation.

Certainly this would appear to be true of those elegant young matrons who are photographed in the glossy magazines, gowned by Balenciaga and coiffed by Alexandre. You would think that merely *looking* like that would require a full forty-hour week of zealous consecration. But no.

"The serene, Botticelli-like beauty of Mrs. William Townsend Heggenworth II," the caption reads, "belies her vibrantly active life. The mother of five exuberant young sons, she is an expert horsewoman, an accomplished painter, a collector of eighteenth-century porcelains and a hard-working member of the Charity Guild. The chatelaine of three homes (an apartment on Central Park West, a château in the Loire Valley and a remodeled lighthouse in the Galápagos), she prefers to entertain at dinner *intime* for eight or ten, often doing much of the cooking herself. Despite her complex, multifaceted life, she maintains an air of detached calm, and she is never too busy to serve as her husband's co-pilot on spur-of-the-moment business trips to London, Hong Kong or Johannesburg."

Now that's a woman who fully embraces the new femininity in a multiplicity of spheres. However does she manage it?

I'm afraid that I myself have made only a marginal adjustment to contemporary womanhood. There are days when I can barely work up enough momentum to curl my eyelashes. Ambition sinks so low that I quail at the prospect of the rich, full, multifaceted day ahead—housework, committee meeting, what-to-have-for-dinner, getting Molly to her swimming lesson and Katie to her orthodontist appointment, trying to find a place to park the car.

Just between us, I have a little secret dream. I know it sounds implausible coming from a member of the indestructible, indefatigable sex, but I have an overwhelming desire to spend a day—a whole, blissful, purposeless day—in bed.

There I'll be, reclining between silken sheets, my head banked by lacy pillows, wearing a filmy blue bed jacket and reading the latest John Cheever. The smells of homemade beef broth and cheese soufflé, being prepared for my lunch, will drift up from the kitchen. The telephone will ring from time to time (I forgot to mention that it's the day of the PTA rummage sale when I'm supposed to be in charge of Women's and Children's Footwear) but it will be answered on the first ring, and a voice from downstairs will explain that Madame is indisposed and can't be disturbed.

It's a modest dream, really. Nothing on the scale of the vision of Kubla Khan. Is it too much to ask? Yes, I'm afraid so.

THREE

CHILDREN! CHILDREN!

See Mommy Run! Run, Mommy, Run!

I have a whole library of books on child psychology, and I refer to them constantly. Scarcely a day goes by that I don't thumb through an index, looking up "Bedtime, resistance to" or "Adolescence, parental rejection during" or "Neatness, lack of in seven-year-olds." And I must admit that I've learned a lot from my reading. It has helped me understand my children.

When Ann, my first-born, was a month and a half old, she slept all day and stayed awake all night. So I bought a book on child care to tell me what to do. After studying a chapter on Behavior Patterns in Infancy, I gained new insights into my child's sleeping habits. True, I was still up at 4 A.M. with a screaming baby, but I was now aware that she wasn't deliberately trying to drive me out of my mind. The condition of my nerves was merely a by-product of her developmental process.

Through the years I have learned to think in terms of Growth Patterns and Underlying Causes. When Katie threw a tantrum because her window shade was crooked, I was aware that this was symptomatic of two-year-old rigidity. And when I discovered Molly squeezing a ribbon of toothpaste down the stairs, through the hall and into the living room, I recognized her behavior as a nonproductive form of self-expression.

It's reassuring to know that when your child screams that she hates you, it doesn't mean she hates you. It means that she's found a verbal outlet for tensional frustration.

And certainly it's comforting to have the assurances of child psychologists that children's abnormal interest in sex is perfectly normal. All schools of thought agree that their questions should be answered calmly and matter-of-factly.

Even so, meticulous adherence to the rules is no guarantee of success. When Molly was five, she asked me how babies were born and I told her. I handled it rather well, if I do say so myself, answering her questions one at a time, simply and directly. No evasions about the stork, and no nonsense about birds and bees. She nodded comprehendingly, and I figured that *that* was *that*. For a while anyway.

Then one night as I was tucking her into bed, she said, "Mommy, why didn't you tell the truth about babies?"

I was stunned. "But I did tell you the truth!" I said. "What did you hear? Who have you been talking to?" Then, remembering that I was supposed to be calm and matter-of-fact, I added, "Tell Mommy about it, darling."

Molly gave me a long, measuring look. "Martha's mother says that the stork brings babies. It carries them in its beak. She showed me a picture of it, so I know it's true. I think it's nice," she added. "A lot nicer than that other way *you* told me about."

Molly got straightened out eventually. By Martha.

A friend of mine had a somewhat different experience. She *did* tell her little boy, Mike, about the stork because she was sure someone would bring it up sooner or later. She told him there was no such thing. To prove her point, she read him a book on reproduction, which included graphic sketches of spermatozoa and Fallopian tubes. Mike was also told that there was no Santa Claus, and he was disabused of any silly ideas he might have picked up about the Easter Bunny and the Tooth Fairy. No fantasy for Mike. He was being brought up to accept the world of reality.

One early November day, when Mike was in the first grade, he came home from school, muttering that his teacher was a dope. She told fibs. His mother pricked up her ears. If that teacher was filling the children's heads with old wives' tales, she was going straight to the school board. "What did your teacher tell you?" she asked.

"Oh, she talked about Thanksgiving," Mike said disgustedly, "and she told us a lot of junk about some people called Pilgrims. *We* don't believe in Pilgrims, do we, Mommy?"

Despite the hazards involved, I wish my children would ask more questions about sex. I seem to be better informed on it than most other subjects. Admittedly, it's unsettling to have my morning reverie over the grocery list interrupted by a piping voice asking, "But how does the Daddy plant the little seed in the Mommy's tummy?"

Still, I do know the answer to this question. What really

unnerves me are the questions to which I don't know answers: What makes an airplane fly? How come you don't like Karmel Korn? If you hadn't married Daddy, whose little girl would I be?

When I discuss the call-girl racket hearings with Ann, I can be perfectly matter-of-fact because I know almost as much about the subject as she does. But I get upset when she questions me about participial clauses and equilateral triangles. And when she tosses me a conversation opener like, "Mommy, what do you think we ought to do about Vietnam?" I mutter that I'm too busy now to discuss it.

Katie's questions are a different type altogether. They're the hypothetical sort that would make Aristotle bite his fingernails. Last week she asked, "If you could choose one number for both your IQ and your weight, what would you pick?" I've been pondering this ever since, and I can't make up my mind. Would I sacrifice my figure for an intelligence quotient of 160? If I could get my weight down to 110, would anything else really matter? Where does true happiness lie?

Lest I've given the impression that I'm the matter-of-fact sort who has no head for abstractions, I hasten to add that I'm just as nonplussed by practical, down-to-earth posers like, "Why do I have to eat my oatmeal?"

Had I not read all those books on child psychology, I would probably answer, "Because I'm your mother and I say so!" But being psychiatrically oriented, I know that children deserve rational explanations for parental directives. And I try, I really do. Just listen to me:

"Because oatmeal is good for you. . . . Because it's hot and nourishing, and it gives you the energy you need to work hard in school. . . . It's not gooshy at all, it's delicious. . . . Of course, I like it. I love it . . . I'd like nothing better, but I'm dieting. . . . No, I don't want you to get fat. . . . I just *told* you why! Because it's full of vitamins. . . . I'm not always talking about how tired I am! . . . When I said I was absolutely exhausted, I didn't mean, I just meant—well, adults get tired in a different way than children do. . . . Oh, all right then, *don't* eat it!"

What makes a performance like this particularly demoralizing is that I keep comparing myself to the mothers I see on television—the ones in those wholesome family programs depicting life in a typical American household. It's not only that TV mothers are prettier, more smartly dressed and better housekeepers than I am (although I do feel ashamed of myself when I compare my around-the-house pedal pushers with their charming at-home outfits, and I can't imagine how they manage to keep their kitchens so immaculate). But the really depressing thing about TV mothers is the marvelous adjustment they've made to parenthood. They're so understanding, so perceptive, so clearly born to be mothers.

When Molly watches that serenely cheerful mother on the Patty Duke show, what must she think of *me?* Katie sees Donna Reed coping calmly and efficiently with staggering domestic crises, and then she observes me, going to pieces over routine mishaps like lost library books and dead goldfish. I know these programs are considered good, wholesome entertainment for children, but I sometimes wonder if "Peyton Place" doesn't perform a more worthwhile service. It certainly does a lot to lift my spirits and assuage my guilt feelings. I may not volunteer to be a Brownie leader, and I refuse to let Molly keep her hamster in the kitchen, but compared to the way those parents in "Peyton Place" carry on, I'm a paragon of motherhood.

I'm afraid, though, that "Peyton Place" came along too late to have much impact on my children's attitude. They developed a distorted view of parenthood during their

formative years when they were reading books like *Fun with Billy and Sue* and *A Day at the Seashore*. In case you're lucky enough to have missed them, these books are realistic, easy-to-read stories about children living everyday lives with their mommies and daddies, who are supposed to be just like mommies and daddies everywhere.

The catch is that Billy and Sue's parents aren't like mommies and daddies everywhere. Anyway, *I've* never met any adults who were as beautifully uncomplicated as all that.

Storybook parents never lose their tempers and yell, "If I've told you once, I've told you a thousand times . . . !" They never snap, "Oh, stop bothering me and go watch the Flintstones!" No sir. They are always cheerful, always patient and ever ready for fun and frolic with the family. A storybook mommy is never too busy to take little Jennifer to the zoo to visit the giraffes. A storybook mommy is willing—nay, eager—to welcome a stray pregnant cat into the household. As for Daddy, a typical chapter, titled "Daddy Can Fix It," should give you a quick idea of what *he's* like.

There has been a lot of alarmism about modern children's lack of respect for their parents, and I place a good share of the blame on those books. How can a child look up to a father who stacks up so poorly against Billy's daddy? My children's father not only can't fix it, he doesn't even want to try.

I sometimes think wistfully of how different everything would be if my children's generation had been raised, as I was, on *Grimm's Fairy Tales*. The parents in Grimm's stories didn't escort their youngsters on educational bus rides and merry excursions to the seashore. They beat their children, fed them on black bread and water and sent them into the forest to starve. Had our children been exposed to Grimm's wicked stepmothers, hardhearted fathers and wrathful nurses, they'd thank their lucky stars to have such wonderfully kind and sympathetic parents.

So why *didn't* I read them *Grimm's Fairy Tales?* For the simple reason that I was trying my darndest to be an exemplary mother. When my children were little, child psychologists held the view that fairy tales were too strong stuff for tender young minds. Fantasy was Out, and everyday realism was In.

Now—now that it's too late—the child psychologists have changed their minds. The latest word is that fantasy and make-believe are beneficial.

As I understand the new theory, fairy tales help children work out their hostilities through imagination. Instead of kicking Mommy in the shins because she won't let them eat cookies before lunch, they can vent their anger by pretending that Mommy is the wicked witch whom Gretel pushed into the oven. While this isn't exactly a reassuring glimpse into the infant mind, it certainly beats getting kicked in the shins and it seems fair enough to me.

What seems *un*fair (indeed, it makes me so cross at the child psychologists that I could grind their bones to make my bread) is that they waited so long to switch signals. It's too late now to introduce my children to the wicked stepmother in "Snow White" and the greedy father in "Rumpelstiltskin."

Still, something must be done to give them a more realistic concept of adult behavior than the goody-goody parents in the Billy and Sue books.

What's needed is a manual to give children some insight into parents and their problems. And here it is—A Child's Guide to Grownups. I offer it in the faint hope that some child might read it under the mistaken impression that it is about sex.

Eating Habits

There's no denying that adults have bizarre tastes in food. They like weird things like mushrooms, hollandaise sauce, pimientos, lobster and asparagus, and they do not appreciate such delicacies as Pronto Pups and cotton candy. Yet they do seem to survive on their strange diet, and it would be advisable for children to adopt a philosophic attitude and refrain from sneering at the icky veal paprika which Mommy and Daddy are eating. Mommy doesn't make gagging noises like that about the peanut butter and marshmallow sandwich which Junior is guzzling down. And she not only has to sit there watching him eat it. She had to steel herself to *fix* it.

Self-discipline

During their early, preparental years, adults acquire a number of selfish habits, such as sleeping through the night and spending their money on themselves. It is the first child's responsibility to re-educate them to a new way of life. Mommy must learn that when Baby wants his bottle, he wants it NOW, and that excuses and apologies are to no avail. Daddy must learn to put aside his dreams of a golf cart when Baby needs a playpen and a little jump chair.

If these early lessons are well taught, Mommy and Daddy should develop the necessary maturity to fight back their tears when Baby's evening romp cancels out their quiet candlelight dinners. But even the best-adjusted parents succumb to occasional tantrums. Should it happen that Daddy cuts loose with oaths and bellows of anguish at being summoned for the fifteenth time in one evening to fetch a dwink of wa-wa, the wise child will table the motion and fall quietly and gracefully to sleep. This is not a propitious moment to insist that Daddy assist the sandman by singing "Old MacDonald Had a Farm."

Intellectual Abilities

Admittedly, adults are woefully uneducated. They're a total loss at parsing sentences. They know nothing about the principal exports of Uruguay. The simplest problem in compound fractions baffles them, and even long division gives them pause. They squirm, chew their pencils and mutter, "Let's see now, how many times does eight go into seventy-four . . . ?"

Their ignorance is shocking, but the compassionate child will hide his dismay and guide them gently into the paths of knowledge by helping them with homework assignments. It is poor policy to assign parents a theme on Greek drama and, leaving them alone with a stack of encyclopedias, disappear upstairs to watch "Hullabaloo." Children should stick around and help. Parents not only need assistance in spelling words like Agamemnon but, being unaware of Miss Toomey's finicky attitude about margins, they may fail to indent properly. If Susie gets a D on that paper, Mommy and Daddy may lose confidence in themselves and quit trying, and their slipshod work habits will go from bad to worse.

Reflexes and Muscular Coordination

Very few adults can touch their toes without bending their knees, and only a small percentage can turn a decent backward somersault. Not many fathers can chin themselves more than twice, and only precocious mothers can throw a ball overhand. Their manual dexterity is very poor. Their handwriting is atrocious, and they're inept at jacks, rarely progressing beyond twosies.

However awkward parents may be, they have a touching desire to be pals to their children, and it is cruel to laugh at them. Adults are sensitive, and ridicule may push them into exertions beyond their capabilities, which may, in turn, result in slipped spinal discs and sprained sacroiliacs. They should be encouraged to participate in ways that are suited to their own age levels. If Daddy wants to join the ball game, let him. But try to keep him safely on the sidelines, blowing whistles and keeping score. What if he does spoil the fun by fussing about rules and good sportsmanship? He needs that all-important feeling of belonging. And at least he isn't likely to require ambulance service.

Emotional Maturity

Mothers cry easily, and fathers throw tantrums over trifles like rusted bikes and busted stereos. All parents are scaredy-cats. They lie awake nights, worrying about germs, college boards, motorcycles, going steady, busy intersections and unchaperoned parties. Children must be cautioned to respect their parents' fears by not riding bikes no-hands when Mommy is watching, and by keeping their diaries locked. Yet parents should not be overprotected. Sooner or later they must stop holding their children's hands when crossing streets, and it's unreasonable to expect kids over ten to cuddle with Mommy during lightning storms.

But one word of caution: *The Monster from Outer Space* is too scary for anyone over eighteen. Don't urge parents to see it. Don't even tell them the story.

Adolescence

Adolescence is a trying time for parents. They can't seem to do anything right. They're terrible drivers. They make embarrassing remarks in front of other people. They don't know anything about clothes, and their musical taste is undeveloped. Worst of all, they poke into things that are none of their business, and are forever asking personal questions: "Where are you going? Who's going with you? When will you be back?"

Patience is the keynote here. Patience and understanding. Parents, during adolescence, suffer from feelings of loneliness and rejection. Admittedly, parents undergoing this difficult transitional stage, have nothing to say that anybody'd be interested in hearing, but an occasional "How's tricks, Mom?" and "How's business, Dad?" will do wonders to boost their morale.

And bear in mind that adolescence does end eventually. Parents snap out of it as time goes on. Many a parent who is a terrible trial during adolescence at, say, thirty-six years of age, turns into quite a decent human being at forty.

Security and Self-confidence

Parents are pitifully insecure, and no wonder! Still, they do have their good points. They're eager to please and willing to learn, and they're touchingly grateful for a word of praise now and then. The important thing is to avoid setting goals for them that are unrealistically high.

Bear in mind that they're adults, and try to be patient with them.

Ballet Lessons, Piano Lessons, French, Badminton,
Modern Dance, Trampoline
and
Other Children's Activities

The problem of which lessons to give which child is as endlessly puzzling as the chicken-or-egg riddle. Should little Emily take piano lessons? French? Modern dance? Ballet? Ice skating? Horseback riding?

Should owlish Osbert be enrolled in the Wednesday afternoon class in Fundamentals of Chess, and rambunctious Robert be signed up for Tumbling and Trampoline? Or vice versa? Who ought to take ballet? Graceful, twinkletoed Lucinda or awkward, flat-footed Betsy?

There are no easy answers to these questions and, the more you ponder them, the more baffled you get. You can study the brochures for guidance, but you won't learn much. All of them (from the gold-crested announcement sent by the Natasha Praskayova School of the Dance to the letter signed by "Uncle" Harry O'Brien at the Sylvan Glade Riding Academy) promise the same long-range fringe benefits: Grace, Poise, Confidence, Wholesome Group Participation and Full Personality Development for the Whole Child.

Certainly you can't leave the choice of lessons up to the children themselves. They either mumble, "Gee, I dunno" or they make preposterous suggestions: "I'd sure like to learn to sky-dive" or "Can I take baton twirling, can I, pleeeze?" The rare child who cries ecstatically, "Oh, I want to take ballet more than anything in the whole world!" makes a mother's heart leap with hope that little Gertrude may be destined to become a prima ballerina. Alas, little Gertrude is not contemplating long hours of practice at the exercise bar. She is imagining herself in white tulle and a rhinestone tiara, floating gracefully through space, and she will be the first member of the class to announce that dancing lessons are stupid and boring.

Fathers are no help at all. "That stuff's a lot of nonsense," they say. "I never took all those lessons when I was a kid, and I turned out okay." A remark like that can lead to a full evening of lively discussion, not necessarily limited to the relative merits of piano, tennis and dancing lessons.

What about other mothers? Can't they be relied on to give realistic appraisals of the classes their children are taking? Unfortunately not. Their primary objective is to enlist new recruits into their car pools. If you tell Susie's mother that you're thinking of enrolling your Amanda in Susie's ballet class, Susie's mother will reply, "Oh, marvelous! I'm sure Amanda will be just as enthusiastic about the class as Susie is!" This testimonial is open to varied interpretation. It could mean that Susie regards that class with the same enthusiasm that she views Brussels sprouts.

In the final analysis, nobody is much help and the decisions are up to you alone. However you arrive at them (I've found that eeny-meeny-miney-mo works as well as any other method) you'll need reasons to explain why you decided as you did, and here's where I can offer some helpful suggestions:

Why should Agnes take piano lessons?
1) Because she shows signs of musical aptitude which ought to be encouraged.
2) Because she's completely uninterested in music.
3) Because there's a piano in the house, and somebody ought to play it.
4) Because there isn't a piano in the house, but a small spinet would look lovely in the bay window.

Why should Tommy take tennis lessons?
1) Because he's terribly awkward and needs to improve his coordination.
2) Because he's so well coordinated that he might turn out to be a second Pancho Gonzales.
3) Because the kid next door is taking tennis lessons.
4) Because someone gave him a tennis racket for his birthday.

Once you have come to a decision, and have your children enrolled in their after-school activities, you may think you can settle back and wait for all that character and cultural development to start showing. It's not quite that simple. There are a number of problems still to be faced.

How to transport your children to and from their classes.
If they can't get there under their own power (and they can't) your Tuesday afternoon schedule may look like this:

Gail's dancing class: 3:30 to 4:30
Michael's tennis class: 4:00 to 5:00
Judy's swimming lesson: 4:15 to 5:00

The tennis courts being a twenty-minute drive from the swimming pool, which is across town from the dance studio, it would be impossible to execute this schedule even if you didn't have to get dinner on the table by 5:30, which you do because your husband has a seven o'clock meeting on Tuesday nights. The obvious solution is to organize a car pool. So you telephone several other mothers whose children are enrolled in your children's classes. They are just as desperate as you, and equally eager to work out a solution.

Millicent's mother will be happy to drive the girls to dancing school if you'll bring them home, but you'll have to switch places on the last Tuesday of the month when her bridge club meets. Sara's mother can drive the children to and from swimming lessons during the month of October, but she won't have any time in November because she's general chairman of the church bazaar. Jeffrey's mother can pick up the boys at the gym on alternate Tuesdays, but she won't be available on the days her cleaning woman comes because she has to drive Mrs. Grimsby to the 5:02 bus. . . .

Possibly, somewhere in this tangled web lies salvation, a workable schedule for all concerned. But who has the mental acuity to figure it out? A friend of mine, a girl of vision and imagination, hit on the answer one evening as her husband was describing the electronic computer that had just been installed in his office.

"You wouldn't believe it!" he marveled. "All you have to do is feed the information into the machine and in seconds it solves problems that would take human beings hundreds of hours to figure out!"

As his wife listened, she was reminded of her own problem—the car-pool dilemma. Surely, she reasoned, if a computer was smart enough to multiply 437,892,735,468 by 982,732,574, it must have the intelligence to work out a pickup-and-delivery schedule for four frantic mothers.

Warming to her subject, she went on to speculate about other services the computer could perform for her. Why, it could not only figure out what to have for dinner and keep track of who had, and hadn't, had chicken pox, but it could also determine whether a giant-size box of detergent weighing 9 pounds, 13 ounces at $2.59 and including a bonus coupon worth 10 cents off the purchase price of the next box, is a better buy than the large economy size, which holds 3 pounds, 2½ ounces, plus a free plastic measuring cup, at 79 cents.

Her husband, clearly a hidebound reactionary, was unreasonably shocked at her suggestion. "Good Lord!" he said. "You can't use a two-million-dollar piece of equipment to solve your petty domestic problems!"

But for his stubbornness, that car pool might have been saved from oblivion. Who knows? It's an idea worth remembering if you should find yourself alone with an idle computer.

How to help your children get the most out of their lessons.

I'm not going to advise you to practice ballet steps and piano scales right along with them. It's a nice idea, of course, but you're busy enough as it is, doing all that chauffeuring. Then, too, you might turn out to be even more inept than your child at *entrechats* and finger exercises.

Even *discussing* those lessons with your child is risky. When your eleven-year-old denounces French lessons as "a big bunch of hooey" your best comeback is, "I don't want to hear any more of that kind of talk. You're going to keep right on taking French, and that's final!" Tempting as it is to rhapsodize on the beauty of the French language

and the Gallic charm of the teacher, Madame LeBlanc—
don't do it. You'll wish you hadn't opened that box of
snakes when your child pounces on you, "Then how come
you don't speak French? Why don't *you* take lessons from
Madame if you think she's so great?"

On the off-chance that you *do* speak French, you'd still
best adopt a hands-off policy toward your youngster's vo-
cabulary lists. *Your* French (be it fluent Parisian or halt-
ing high school) isn't the same language as Madame's,
and you will only supply your youngster with additional
proof that French is a big bunch of hooey.

Still, mothers do have a useful role to play. They should
make absolutely sure that their children realize what lessons
they are taking. Many mothers take this basic point for
granted, not realizing that a child who is participating in a
number of activities may become confused.

Six-year-old Rachel is a case in point. Her mother, who
was entertaining a group of ladies at lunch, gave an enthusiastic report of Rachel's French class. Although the
child had taken only four lessons, she had already learned
a number of words and phrases, and her accent was
remarkably good. "It's very important to start early," her
mother said complacently. "Young children pick up lan-
guages so naturally."

Half an hour later Rachel came home from school. Her
mother said, "Darling, I've been telling the ladies about
your French class. I'm sure they'd like to hear you say
something in French."

Rachel rubbed one foot against the other and said,
"Huh?"

Her mother smiled encouragingly. "Why don't you tell
us your name and how old you are. Remember? *Je
m'appelle* . . ."

Rachel looked at her mother in surprise. "Oh," she said,
"is that *French?* I thought that was *badminton!*"

How to accept defeat gracefully.

A few months ago I met a bright-eyed young mother who should serve as an inspiring example to us all. She and I sat next to each other on folding chairs, waiting for our second graders' interpretive dance class to begin. We got acquainted by asking each other, "Which one is yours?" Mine was Molly, the one in the blue leotard, sitting on the floor biting her toenails. Hers was Charlotte, the one in bright pink, hovering in the doorway to the cloakroom.

"Attention, class!" called the teacher, clapping her hands. "Let's begin by pretending we're maple trees, losing our leaves in the autumn. Let's all spread our branches and flutter, flutter, flutter in the wind."

The children flapped their arms and giggled self-consciously. All except Charlotte, who continued to stand in the doorway, examining a bandage on her thumb. The teacher called to her, "Come, Charlotte! Don't you want to be a maple tree like the other children?"

Charlotte shook her head. Then she ran to her mother, buried her face in Mommy's lap and burst into tears. "I don't want to be a tree!" she sobbed. "I want to go home!"

Her mother patted her head and said, "All right, home we go!" Then she turned to me and said calmly, "Charlotte has made a valuable discovery in this class. I feel that we've got our money's worth."

Aware that they had some sixteen dollars' worth of unused lessons, I was puzzled. "You have?" I asked. "How come?"

"Why, we've learned that modern dance is not Charlotte's forte," she said cheerfully, "and now we're free to explore other possibilities."

I'll admit that we all can't be as chin-up about unamortized sixteen-dollar investments as Charlotte's mother. I happen to be the chin-down type myself, and perhaps you are, too.

Still, there come moments when there seems to be no alternative to letting six of the ten lessons you paid for in advance go unused. There you are, piloting a car with five children in the back seat through 5:30 rush hour traffic, which moves approximately two inches every six minutes. The spareribs for dinner should have gone into the oven half an hour ago, and now you'll have to stop at the store for lamb chops because you have to get to a 7:30 PTA meeting. As you fight off an overwhelming impulse to lay your head on the steering wheel and sob, the children swarm over the back seat, yelling that they hate and despise dancing lessons, that the teacher is a dumb nut, that they haven't learned a single solitary thing and why, why, *why* must they keep on going to that silly, stupid, dumb, boring, icky class?

So *now* what? You are faced with the choice of reliving this ordeal every Thursday for the next six weeks or kissing off the remaining lessons and the fifteen dollars you paid for them.

I hesitate to mention it, but there is a third choice open to you. Mind you, this is only a suggestion, but you might consider it. *If* the teacher is willing, and *if* the other children's mothers are amenable and *if* the class under consideration isn't too strenuous for your age group, you might consider using up those lessons yourself.

I know a group of mothers who get together every week to study French under the tutelage of a delightful Frenchwoman. They've been meeting faithfully every Wednesday morning for three years now, and they're so enthusiastic over their progress that they're planning a group trip to Europe next summer. And it all started with the collapse of their third graders' conversational French class.

So you see? Things can work out nicely after all.

Confidentially, I've been taking a ceramics course since last March when my middle daughter, Katie, announced that she was bored silly making stupid old pots and wanted to go to charm school instead. She not only had five lessons to go, but she had a big bucket of perfectly good clay which I hated to see go to waste.

I won't say that I'm a second Jacob Epstein, but I will say that I'm enjoying the Group Participation, the Fulfillment of Self-Expression and the Satisfaction of Creative Endeavor. And what's more, I have a whole bunch of charming—if slightly lopsided—pots and ashtrays that I made with my own two hands.

As for Grace, Poise, Self-Confidence and Full Personality Development, I expect to acquire them when I start charm school.

FOUR

MEN, WOMEN, MARRIAGE AND ALL THAT

How to Tell a Man from a Woman

What is a man? A man is a creature of superlative intelligence who can understand the principle of jet propulsion, the pari-mutuel betting system and the Dow Jones Averages. He can recall the score of the Army-Navy game in '54, the electoral votes the Republicans won in the last election and the gas mileage of the first car he ever owned. But he can't remember what size socks he wears, the ages of his children or the name of that old Cole Porter number that his wife refers to as "our" song.

And what is a woman? A woman is a rattlebrain who can't read a slide rule, can't follow a road map and is vague about the make and model of the car she drives. But she can recall in vivid detail the yellow organdy dress she wore to her high school prom, and she can mentally multiply sixteen people by two and one half cheese canapés apiece while she's (a) rolling out pastry, (b) helping one child compose a letter telling Vassar why it's the college of her choice and (c) playing second banana to another child who's asking riddles. ("Of course I'm listening to you, darling. You said that the moron put his father into the refrigerator because he wanted cold pop. That's very clever.")

A man has astonishing manual dexterity. He can light a match on his fingernail. He can untangle a hopelessly snarled fishing line. He can repair a light cord, fix a carburetor, operate a power saw and maneuver a seventeen-foot car into a sixteen-foot parking space. In her wildest dreams a woman couldn't do anything like that. But she can hang up a bathtowel so that the monogram is right side out and precisely centered. She can unjam a stuck zipper. She can construct a pincurl and remove a sliver and balance a plate of food on her lap.

A man has executive ability and unerring judgment. He can make instantaneous decisions about mergers and advertising campaigns, cutbacks in production and million-dollar bond issues. But he has to appeal to his wife (that little muddlehead who can't figure out how much to tip a bellboy) to help him decide which necktie to wear with his gray suit. Faced with a Continental menu, he shrugs helplessly and asks, "Honey, do I like bouillabaisse?"

A man is stoical about lightning and rattlesnakes and spiders. He is fearless about guns and one-engine planes and he'd give his eyeteeth to be an astronaut. He has tremendous physical endurance, and thinks it's great sport to spend all day in a freezing duck blind.

A woman is a timorous creature who lies awake hearing strange noises after reading a news bulletin that a psychopathic killer has escaped from a prison fifteen hundred miles away. But she doesn't quail in terror from a new baby, she'll brave the rigors of a January white sale, and she has an adventurous attitude toward unidentifiable hors d'oeuvres. Stamina? Well, you won't catch her sighing for a go at Everest or volunteering to ride the rapids in a birchbark canoe. But could a man undergo the torments of plucking his eyebrows? Shopping all day in high heels? Sleeping on brush hair curlers?

It is a known fact that men are practical, hard-headed realists, in contrast to women, who are romantic dreamers and actually believe that estrogenic skin cream must do *something* or they couldn't charge sixteen dollars for that little tiny jar. When a woman stares into space with narrowed eyes, there's no telling what flights of fancy might be going on in her head. Of course, that faraway look in her eye could merely indicate that she's wondering what to have for dinner or toying with the idea of letting her bangs grow out. But then again, she might be indulging in a wildly fantastic daydream.

The words "Dear, I've been thinking . . ." strike terror in a husband's soul. But, oblivious to his alarm, she plunges ahead, ". . . if we'd knock out the partition between the kitchen and the back porch, we'd have plenty of space to put in a washer and dryer. Actually, it would be quite a simple—"

"For Pete's sake!" her husband gasps, lowering his newspaper and raising his eyebrows. "You can't go tearing out partitions anywhere you please! You've got to consider the joists! They're what hold up the house, you know."

As a matter of fact, she *didn't* know. But, having been enlightened, she can only be grateful that her practical, down-to-earth husband recognizes her wistful little dream for the crazy, harebrained scheme it really is. Were it not for his superior common sense and technical know-how, she might heedlessly have reduced their nice Dutch colonial to a pile of rubble.

Still, it must be admitted that a man occasionally gets a faraway look in his eye, too. And in fairness, we should tune in on a brief report from *his* secret dream world:

"Honey," he says as he gazes thoughtfully out the window at the autumn leaves piled ankle deep on the front lawn, "you know what we ought to do? We ought to sell the house, buy a trailer, pack up the kids and get the heck out of the whole damned, status-conscious, upward mobility, air-polluted rat race! Just take off like vagabonds for a year or so. You know, like Steinbeck did in *Travels with Charley*. . . ."

As he continues in this vein, waving his arms and babbling incoherencies about sleeping under the stars, Walden Pond, talking to *real* people, teaching his kids to make willow whistles and the possibility of *Life* magazine financing their adventure in exchange for exclusive picture rights, it is difficult to recognize him as the prudent householder who demands itemized bills. His wife may be hard put to know what to say.

Of course, she *could* ask, "Have you been drinking?" and she could remind him of a detail or two (like the children's tendency toward car sickness) that seem to have slipped his mind. But such a wet-blanket approach would only incite him to fling back accusations: "The trouble with you is, you haven't any imagination!" And this, in turn, would lead to tears and recriminations.

A wife would do better to say, "Darling, what a marvelous

idea! I feel exactly the same way myself." She might even go so far as to add, "I'll put the house up for sale first thing in the morning."

She needn't worry that her enthusiasm will encourage him to take positive action and start scouting around for a trailer. She can rest assured that by the next morning all thoughts of Walden Pond will be erased from his mind, and he'll be his old normal self again, scowling over the financial page and reminding her to be sure to call the plumber. But because she's a woman, she won't understand, and she'll eye him across the breakfast table with a puzzled frown.

Men and women can hardly be blamed for finding each other bewildering.

A woman can only marvel at a man's financial acumen. With paper, pencil and patient logic, a man can prove the folly of transferring a savings account from one bank to another in order to get a $3.95 set of steak knives absolutely free. But he can use the same paper and pencil to prove that buying a new car is cheaper in the long run than replacing a cracked windshield on the old car.

Or take instinctual behavior. A man has a sixth sense which enables him to find his way through the cloverleaf, under the overpass, over the viaduct and straight east to the airport without making a single wrong turn, in plenty of time to meet the 10:35 from Seattle. His wife has a sixth sense that prompts her to keep telling him, "George, I have a funny feeling that we're headed in the wrong direction for the airport." But a woman can find the adhesive tape on the bottom shelf of the medicine cabinet, and she has an uncanny intuitive sense that tells her the baby is crying for his Teddy bear and the baby-sitter can't find it.

To make the whole sexual situation even more perplexing, men and women don't even speak the same language. To illustrate, let's ask a husband and wife the same questions and listen to their answers:

What's wrong with the car?
Him: "I think the trouble is in the generator. The brushes are probably worn or the voltage regulator is set too low. The ammeter shows that it isn't charging properly."
Her: "I press on the little doohicky, and it won't start."

How was the movie?
Her: "Marvelous! It's a witty, sophisticated comedy. I'm still chuckling over the dialogue, and the interiors and the clothes are stunning. But for heaven's sake, time your arrival so you don't have to sit through the second feature. It's a horror. One of those dreadful James Bond things, full of sex and violence, and a ridiculous plot. . . ."
Him: "It's the best James Bond yet! There's a shark scene that had me on the edge of my seat but laughing at the same time, y'know. Be sure to miss the second feature, though. It's a dog. Another one of those Italian jobs, filmed in slow motion. . . ."

Where are you going on your vacation this year?
Him: "Well, we don't have any definite plans yet, but I read about this lake basin at eighty-five hundred feet in the High Sierras. Snow-capped peaks on three sides and you won't see another soul for days at a time. You pack in on horseback, and take just bacon and beans and a fly rod. You don't need much because you can practically live on fish. The lakes are thick with golden rainbows and brook trout. Talk about paradise!"
Her: "Well, we don't have any definite plans yet, but the Grays went to this divine resort near Palm Springs. The cabanas are elegant, and the service is too. They even bring you breakfast in bed. The cuisine is French, and the

place is crawling with celebrities. I imagine it's expensive, but I do feel that a vacation is one time when you ought to lap up a bit of glamor, don't you?"

Were you surprised to hear about the Lawsons' divorce?
Her: "I'm only surprised it didn't happen a long time ago. I can't imagine how Ethel put up with Joe all those years. You know how antisocial he is, and he never did a thing to help her around the house. Why, she actually had to spade the flower beds herself, as if she didn't have enough to do, being president of the Auxiliary and everything. That's another thing about Joe. He never gave Ethel credit for anything. Instead of being proud of her community activities, he made fun of her. Joe's trouble is that he's emotionally immature, and he felt threatened by Ethel's accomplishments. And what's more . . ."
Him: "Surprised? Hell, no! The way that woman nagged poor old Joe . . ."

How did your redecorating turn out?
Her: "Oh, we're thrilled with it! The walls and draperies are bone white, and the sofa is upholstered in emerald-green linen. We built floor-to-ceiling bookcases on the south wall, and I found a darling Victorian loveseat, upholstered in lime velvet. . . ."
Him: "It cost twice as much as we figured, and now there isn't a decent place to read in the whole room."

What did you think of the triple play in the game last night?
Him: "Say, wasn't that something! You don't see a play like that more than twice in a lifetime! Top of the ninth, nobody out and the Sox are hanging onto a one-run lead. The first two Bisons get singles, and then Martinelli hits this screaming liner right into Joey Murawski's glove! He tags up, and the peg to second is perfect! Beautiful!"
Her: "Triple play?"

What did they serve for dinner?

Her: "The most marvelous paella, made with shrimp and clams and Italian sausage and chicken. It was seasoned with an unusual herb, and flavored with white wine. It looked gorgeous, too, served in an enormous French casserole."

Him: "Rice and fish and stuff, all gucked up together."

Was it a pretty wedding?

Her: "Exquisite! It was an all-white wedding, flawless in every detail. The flower arrangements were breathtaking, and the food was elegant. I took mental notes through the whole affair because it's the sort of wedding I'd like my own daughters to have when the time comes."

Him: "The champagne alone must have cost poor Herb a small fortune. Believe you me, I'm not going to throw a blowout like that for my kids. I'm going to buy them a ladder, and help them elope."

Have you seen the new baby?

Her: "Oh, he's precious! He has enormous dark eyes, and the sweetest little rosebud mouth and adorable fat cheeks. His hair was black at birth, but now it's coming in blond, and I wouldn't be surprised if it turned out to be curly. His name is Charles, but they call him Chuckie."

Him: "I think it's a girl."

Marriage—American Style

Is my marriage a success? Are my husband and I compatible? Did I marry the right man? Am I a good wife? Alas, the answer to all these questions is NO.

Every time I add up my score in one of those "Are You Happily Married?" quizzes, I discover that my marriage doesn't even qualify as a failure. It's a disaster. If I'm honest, I can't answer a single one of those questions right. I can't even answer them right if I'm *dis*honest.

Question: Do you share mutual interests?

Answer: No. His passion in life is fishing. I hate wading in cold, wet water. He likes movies about spies and airplanes, and I like movies about rich people. We both like to play bridge, but not with each other. His Thelonius Monk records give me a headache. I like Gilbert and Sullivan.

Q. What first attracted you to each other?

A. We both liked the works of an obscure poet (I can't remember his name) whom practically nobody else had ever heard of. I doubt if this would have been much of a magnet, though, if we'd belonged to the same sex.

Q. Did your families approve of your marriage?

A. No. My mother thought he wasn't good enough for me, and his mother thought I wasn't good enough for him. It's hard to say who was right.

Q. Do you have the same basic concerns and attitudes?

A. I wouldn't go so far as to say *that*. Naturally, we share a lot of concerns: the children, the bank statement, the downspouts, the puddle the puppy made in the front hall, the grocery bills and the brown spots on the rhododendron leaves. But our attitudes toward them rarely coincide.

Q. Are you in fundamental agreement on family finances?

A. Well, we both deplore extravagance. He deplores mine and I deplore his.

Q. Do you take offense easily?

A. What's "easily"? I asked him if he thought I looked funny in hip-rider pants, and he said yes.

Q. Do you have a common goal in life?

A. We'd both like to be very, very rich. But we'll never succeed because we married each other.

Q. Does he do things that get on your nerves?

A. I'll say he does! He steams up the bathroom mirror when he takes a shower. He plays the hi-fi so loud he can't even hear me scream at him to turn it down. He leaves apple cores in ashtrays. When I hand him the newspaper

I'm reading to show him an interesting item, he *keeps* it. When I'm engrossed in a detective story, he reads editorials aloud to me.

Q. Do you feel that your role as a mother and homemaker is beneath you?

A. No. I feel it's beyond me.

Q. Do little things irritate him?

A. The littlest things you ever heard of. Dripping stockings hanging over the shower rod. Misplaced car keys. Telephone receivers left off the hook. Creamed vegetables. Traffic citations. Starched shirt collars. Things like that.

Q. Do you try to create a serene and relaxed atmosphere in your home?

A. I have three children, a neurasthenic cocker spaniel, a loud Siamese cat, two television sets, a piano and three radios tuned to different stations. Nothing short of general anesthesia would create a serene atmosphere around our house.

Q. Does it make you angry when your husband spends an occasional evening playing poker with the boys?

A. Not when he wins.

Q. Do you encourage him in his work or profession?

A. I do my best. I keep telling him he ought to get a raise.

Q. Do you enjoy talking to each other?

A. Oh, we enjoy talking to each other all right. The problem is listening to each other.

Q. Do you take an interest in his health?

A. I warn him not to catch cold when he goes fishing. I read articles about cholesterol and I shake my head when he orders apple pie à la mode. I tell him he worries too much.

Q. Do you and your husband present a united front in disciplining your children?

A. More or less. We both agree that the children stay

up too late, eat too much candy and don't study hard enough. Now if we could only convince the children . . .

Q. Are you able to compromise when you disagree?

A. The other night we decided to go to the movies. He wanted to see *Goldfinger*. I was dying to see *The Yellow Rolls-Royce*. So we went to a Japanese movie with English subtitles, which neither of us much wanted to see. I guess you could call this a compromise.

Q. When you go to extra trouble to add gracious little touches around your home, does he notice your efforts?

A. Oh, he notices all right. If I sprinkle herbs in the stew, he asks why it tastes funny. The other night I put those cute little frilly things on the ends of the lamb chops and he said—well, I can't repeat what he said.

Q. Do you take pains to make yourself as attractive for your husband as you do for a party?

A. Oh, come now! Let's not be silly.

Q. Do you bolster each other's confidence?

A. I tell him that anyone with his brains and ability ought to be able to hook my dress in back. He tells me that anybody—even a mechanical moron like me—can learn to change a fuse.

Q. Does he show an interest in the things that are important to you?

A. Last night, as I was describing a darling chiffon dress I saw in a shop window, he interrupted to ask, "Did you remember to get the oil changed in the car?"

Q. Do you show an interest in the things that are important to him?

A. No, I don't. I have more important things on my mind than trout flies and lube jobs.

Q. When things go wrong, do you blame each other?

A. Not always. Sometimes we blame the children. Sometimes we blame Congress. Sometimes we just rail at fate or sulk.

Q. Do you believe that you and your husband have a mutually satisfying relationship, based on understanding, love and respect?

A. We-ell, I don't think about it in precisely those terms, but before taking this test I figured we were getting along pretty well. Now, after totting up my marriage score, it's clear that my husband and I are the most mismatched couple since the Owl and the Pussycat. Yet here we are, with three children, a joint bank account and all that monogrammed silver. So what's the solution?

The experts have a ready answer: Adjust. This sounds deceptively easy, like those ads that say, "No money down and small monthly payments." What adjustment actually means is, you're supposed to turn yourself into someone else who doesn't resemble you at all. You must be even-tempered, cheerful, considerate, calm, dependable and, above all, emotionally mature. Once you've accomplished that, you will be rewarded with a truly adult and meaningful marriage. In addition, the experts hint, you may even attain the ultimate prize—sexual fulfillment. Hint nothing! They come right out and say so. This puzzles me. Whatever gave them the idea there was anything amiss in *that* department?

I can't understand why everyone nowadays has such a low opinion of marital sex. The marriage experts apparently believe that nine out of ten married couples find it easier to get the kids to bed than to lure each other there—a disheartening point of view which is wholeheartedly supported by contemporary novelists and playwrights, who itemize in clinical detail the woes and frustrations of conjugal lovemaking.

Oddly enough, one never reads about an *un*married couple having any problems of sexual adjustment. Unlike Mr. and Mrs., who just can't seem to get the hang of it, the unmarried take to sex like ducks to water and unfailingly achieve perfect union in a star-spangled blaze of glory. Indeed, they are so absorbed in the throbbing, pulsating, all-consuming intensity of passion that they never give a moment's thought to anything else. If they aren't actually *in* bed, they're daydreaming of the last time or planning the program for the next time. It's hard to understand how they keep body and soul together. Don't they ever get haircuts? Pick up clothes at the dry cleaner's? Watch TV? Remember to register and vote?

Evidently not. Unmarried lovers lead remarkably uncomplicated lives both in and out of bed. They exist in a rarefied stratosphere, unmarred by the little domestic difficulties that plague marriage. You never read of an unmarried couple running out of cigarettes or losing the car keys. And they never, never, *never* disagree about what time is bedtime. It *always* is.

Everyone seems to agree that sex comes naturally to the unmarried, but married couples make estranged bedfellows. If that awful truth is true, the solution is both obvious and simple. Don't get married.

A more complicated solution would be to go ahead and get married. Then, after an orientation period, during which your problems build up into a Wall of Hostility, consult your yellow pages for the name of a marriage counselor and dump the whole sorry mess in *his* lap.

There is some risk involved in taking this step. If the counselor should perform a particularly successful salvage job on your marriage, you might find your case history splashed across the pages of a national magazine; and even though it didn't identify you by name, wouldn't you feel kind of funny? I mean, imagine seven million people reading a step-by-step résumé of your wedding night! On the other hand, I guess you might feel a sense of mission and take quiet pride in making a contribution to scientific knowledge—like that doctor in *Yellow Jack* who let himself get bitten by an infected mosquito.

These marital case histories are absorbing reading, and they serve an educational purpose. Through illuminating glimpses into other people's troubled marriages, the reader gains insight into her own problems. To illustrate, let's look at a case of incompatibility and see what we can learn from it:

The wife lists her grievances. She complains that her husband not only refuses to carry out the garbage and never refills ice trays, but she suspects that he is paying the rent for a redhead. The husband tells his side of the case. His wife has lost all pride in her appearance, weighs one hundred and seventy-six pounds and is a sloppy housekeeper. Furthermore, she rebuffs his advances on the pretext that she can't go to bed until she has pasted her U.S. commemoratives in her stamp album.

The prospects for saving this marriage would appear to be fairly thin. But with the aid of a marriage counselor, the couple comes to realize that their problems stem from emotional immaturity. The wife discovers that she left the dinner dishes unwashed because of her basic resentment at being born a female. The husband learns that he refused to carry out the garbage because of his childhood feelings of rejection, caused by wearing his older brother's hand-me-downs.

After learning to discuss their hostilities freely and frankly, and strengthened by new insights, the husband and wife embark on a joint self-improvement program. The wife slims down to a size nine, the loose stamps are used for postage, the redhead is traded for a garbage disposal and—when last seen—the happy couple are cozily analyzing their personalities as a preliminary warm-up for bedtime.

Thought-provoking, isn't it? By the time you're halfway through one of these little dramas, you're likely to find yourself eyeing your own marriage and examining your psyche and your husband's psyche for buried hostilities.

Why did he track mud into the front hall last night? Was he subconsciously punishing you for overcooking his breakfast egg? And why *did* you serve him that cellophane-edged horror? Were you unconsciously retaliating for his refusal to go to the PTA meeting the night before? And what about that time you went to the rest room in the gas station and he drove off without you? Did he simply forget that you were with him? Or was he expressing an unconscious desire to be rid of you? You dislike darning his socks? Could this mean that you have ambivalent feelings about your female role and—oh dear, let's stop this. I mustn't encourage you to think such depressing thoughts.

As a matter of fact, I think I'll quit tormenting myself with disturbing questions about my own marriage. From now on I'm going to give it the benefit of the doubt and assume that it *is* a success, no matter how much evidence I read to the contrary. I don't *care* if my marital IQ is dangerously low. What if there are a few unresolved conflicts in my marriage? Is there anything so terrible about a little emotional immaturity?

I'm not sure that I want a genuinely adult, perfectly integrated, beautifully attuned relationship with my husband anyway. It sounds like a terribly demanding way of life, and not much fun.

I give up trying to perfect my marriage into an idyllic relationship, and I think I'll just leave those little molehills *be*. Okay, so we're not an ideal couple, like Mickey and Jayne. But then, come to think of it, neither are *they*.

FIVE

WHO? ME? PAMPERED?

Grandma, Grandma, I've Been Thinking

No, I don't thank my lucky stars that I'm not my poor old-fashioned grandmother, who scrubbed clothes on a washboard and mopped floors on her hands and knees. I doubt that Grandma would jump at the chance to be *me*.

Sure, she'd marvel at my automatic washing machine and my instant furniture polish in the spray can. I marvel at them myself. But my life isn't the gay, carefree existence pictured in the dishwasher advertisements. And even though

I'm the proud owner of an electric floor polisher, I still need a drink before dinner.

I need a nap, too, although I can't find time to take one—and this puzzles me. People are always saying that I, the modern American homemaker, have oodles of work-free hours to spend as I please. If I added up all the seconds, minutes and hours that modern work-savers are supposed to liberate for me each day, I'd have more free time than the day has.

Well, if I've got it, where *is* it? Some days I'm so rushed that I can't find time to push back my cuticle.

I wouldn't mind being busy and harried if I didn't have to pretend that I'm not, if I could moan and complain about it. But I'm a modern American homemaker, and I've forfeited my right to grumble. That's why I don't thank my lucky stars that I'm not Grandma. When she felt like a tired housewife, she could *act* like a tired housewife. No one would have dared to suggest that she wasn't a hard-working, self-sacrificing woman who toiled ceaselessly to keep her home and her family in order. Grandpa knew it. Her children knew it. Everyone knew it. She herself had no doubts about her essential worth and importance.

Enthroned in such security, Grandma could afford the luxury of *not* complaining. Everyone was already sorry for her.

As for me, everyone knows that I am a pampered female who spends her days languidly pushing buttons that set automatic household servants in motion. My husband knows it only too well. If I should complain that I am all worn out, he would stare at me in amazement. What have I done to wear myself out? Doesn't my glide-easy vacuum with the self-winding cord eliminate dust and dirt as if by magic? Isn't my freezer stocked with TV dinners? Don't my miracle detergents dissolve dirt and grease in seconds, yet leave my hands soft and smooth? Why, I even have an electric can opener!

Just between us, I'm sometimes puzzled myself. Why *isn't* my life the relaxed, carefree existence it's cracked up to be?

The obvious answer is that it's my own fault, that I am an inefficient, inept, flutterbrained creature who can't cope. Or—even worse—that I am a neurotic malcontent who enjoys feeling persecuted.

Of course, in my saner moments, I don't really believe that. No, the real answer is that modern homemaking is a demanding, exasperating way of life, fraught with booby traps disguised as blessings.

Now I'm not advocating that we trade in our dial-aumatic washers for scrubboards and go back to Grandma's era. That would not only be silly but unpatriotic. We've got to think of the economy of the country, which depends on us to trade in our old washing machines for newer and snazzier models. No, we'd better keep things the way they are. But let's knock off the burbling, starry-eyed enthusiasm and take a good, clear look at the way things *really* are.

Let's start by focusing on the loose talk that's floating around:

"Machines do all the work nowadays. Women don't do anything but push buttons."

Like most absurd ideas, this one contains a germ of truth. The automatic washing machine does wash, rinse and spin-dry the laundry at the turn of a dial, and the automatic dryer fluff-dries it to perfection. They're marvelous machines, no doubt about it. Indeed, washing the modern way is so easy that it's pointless to think twice before tossing last night's almost-clean tablecloth in the wash. Luckily, it's made of no-iron fabric, so it doesn't need any, well, *hardly* any, ironing.

Then, too, it's pretty difficult to dredge up a justifiable excuse for sending anything (including men's shirts and ruffled curtains) to the laundry. The laundry, of course, not only washes and dries, but starches, irons, folds, mends and sews on buttons. Still, when a lady has all that modern equipment of her own, is this a reasonable excuse? Any way you look at it (and I, personally, have lain awake nights looking at it every which way) it's a moral dilemma.

At times like that, I often think about my grandmother. It's true that her laundry facilities were primitive. She had to make do with an old-fashioned washboiler and a scrubboard. And an old-fashioned Norwegian lady who came in twice a week to do the laundry.

This same lady came to help the cook wash dishes when Grandma had company for dinner. Naturally, I don't need help when I have a dinner party because I have an automatic dishwasher. I'm lucky, I know that. But there are times—say at 1:30 in the morning, after the guests have departed, and I'm standing at the sink scraping shrimp curry and chocolate sauce off plates and loading them into the dishwasher—well, at times like that I don't give thanks that I'm me and not Grandma.

"Everything is so much easier than it used to be."

Right. And a lot of things might better have been left difficult, if you ask my opinion, which nobody ever does. (Who *are* those women who get queried by housewife-opinion polls, anyway?)

Take wallpapering. Back in the days before they invented precut, easy-hang wallpaper, you had to hire a professional paperhanger. Now it's such a cinch that we, us pampered housewives, can scamper up the ladder and do it ourselves. We can shampoo our own rugs with quick 'n' easy carpet-cleaning solutions, and touch up our silverware with our little replating kits. We can change a flat tire ourselves, now that we've been blessed with the hydraulic jack.

Tough jobs that used to be way beyond a woman's capabilities are now well within the feminine province. Now perhaps this isn't so awful. Indeed, we might take a certain tight-lipped satisfaction in our self-reliance. It would be ego-building to think of ourselves as gallant, spunky pioneer types, performing hard, masculine jobs with our own two hands. That's a self-image we could learn to live with.

The trouble is, they've got a countertrend operating that makes us look like lazy good-for-nothings. What they've done is to take all the work out of jobs that weren't much work in the first place. Now that milk is homogenized, we needn't shake milk bottles. We don't have to shell peas or string beans or squeeze oranges because modern freezing has relieved us of those tasks. The electric can opener has liberated us from the job of turning that little lever by hand. Now there's an electric salad-tosser on the market. And an automatic letter-opener.

Any day now I expect to read advertisements hailing two sensational new boons to womankind: (1) an automatic pillow-plumper ("Plump pillows the easy, modern, scientific way!") and (2) a lightweight cement mixer in a choice of eight decorator colors ("So easy to operate even a woman can do it!").

Given a choice, I'd rather plump pillows the hard way than mix cement the easy way.

"Cooking is a lost art."
If cooking is a lost art, who's buying all the fancy cookbooks that are published nowadays? Professional chefs? No indeed. They're *writing* them. They're confessing their trade secrets so housewives like you and me can whip up

lobster Pavillon and sole Marguery and strawberries Romanoff in our kitchens.

Okay, so we're also buying canned cream sauce and instant mashed potatoes and precooked rice. Yes, and frozen dinners, too. And very handy they are, I must say. There are days in every woman's life when dinnertime arrives before the breakfast dishes are done. Maybe she has spent the day in a committee meeting, revising bylaws. Maybe all the children are in bed with the chicken pox. Maybe (I've *got* to admit this) she has played canasta all afternoon or spent the day shopping for a lampshade to match the blue dot in the bedroom wallpaper.

On such occasions the modern housewife may dump a can of tuna fish into a can of cream sauce, throw in a package of frozen peas and call it dinner. And why not? She'd be foolish not to use emergency rations in an emergency.

But there are other times—say, an ordinary, run-of-the-mill day, when she has plenty of time to cook dinner. *Now* let's observe the modern housewife in action. What is she doing? Why, she's opening a can of cream sauce! Wouldn't you think she'd be ashamed of herself? She has time to make her own cream sauce, and there's nothing very difficult about . . .

But wait a minute! *Now* what is she doing? She's adding white wine to the cream sauce and beating in a couple of egg yolks and some kind of herb. Now she's pouring the whole business over something—it looks like scallops—and arranging mushrooms around them, and sprinkling grated cheese around . . . why, for goodness sakes, she's making Coquilles St. Jacques!

How often did Grandma make Coquilles St. Jacques, hmm?

Now I wouldn't for the world knock Grandma's cooking. Her chicken fricassee was out of this world. Her marrowbone dumplings and her apple pandowdy melted in your mouth. On the other hand, some of the things *we* cook would have struck Grandma as mighty fancy fare: beef stroganoff, veal scallopini, sukiyaki, paella, pot au feu, Caesar salad, crepes suzettes, zabaglione. . . .

It's true that cooking isn't what it was in Grandma's day, but Grandma's cooking wasn't like this either. And why should it be? Cooking, like fashion, changes with the world we live in. Grandma set the best table she could in her day. And so do we, in ours.

It took Grandma several washings to get the sand out of her spinach, and she had to chop it by hand. We buy spinach already cleaned in little freezer cartons, and we puree it in the electric blender. This saves us quite a hunk of time, enough to make spinach soufflé. Even if we season it with instant onion (and we do) it still takes some doing.

We hate to admit it. We like to pretend that it's no trouble at all. "Oh, I just throw a bunch of stuff into a casserole and pop it in the oven!" we say airily.

Now, saying this to another woman is perfectly safe. She knows it's a lie, and you know that she knows it's a lie. Actually, it's a formalized ritual, and a hostess who is so gauche as to admit that she spent the whole day in the kitchen might as well turn in her satin hostess pants for a cotton housedress.

Still, I'm afraid we've gone too far. We're going to have to forsake sophistry and start telling the truth. Some people (men, for example) actually believe all that nonsense. It's time to blurt out the facts boldly and frankly: beef bourguignon is a hell of a lot of work.

"Keeping a house spick-and-span is a cinch nowadays."
You know who's to blame for this nutty idea? Those demented housewives on TV commercials, that's who. You've seen them—the hysterics who burble with rapture

over their sparkling sinks, which have been treated with Poof! (the jiffy, no-rub dirt chaser with miracle enzyme action); the idiotic mothers who beam sunnily when Junior knocks over a glass of milk because now they can have another go at the linoleum with revolutionary, self-polishing Wax-O, which makes floors shine, shine, shine!; the languorous beauties who purr lovingly over their pastel-colored vacuum cleaners with eight separate attachments. There's something downright Freudian about the breathless way they murmur over those machines, the tenderness with which they caress those attachments.

But why go on? You've seen them. You know what they're like. And, unfortunately, so do your husband and children. This is the crux of the problem. Your loved ones, who lead sheltered lives and don't know any better, get the idea that those lunatics on TV are *normal*. Then they start wondering what's wrong with *you*. How come *you* never enthuse over your miracle detergents? Why don't *you* smile and sing when you wash windows the modern way? Why do you gnash your teeth over spilled milk? What's wrong with you, anyway? Maybe you ought to see a psychiatrist.

Well, maybe consulting a psychiatrist isn't such a bad idea at that. At least he'd *listen* when we try to explain that science and engineering have not taken all the housework out of housework.

We, us modern homemakers, are expected to maintain a standard of cleanliness that was impossible in Grandma's day. Now, thanks to science, it's merely *next* to impossible —which means that we have to stay right in there and pitch. Housewives could be philosophic about grease-spattered ovens until someone invented quick 'n' easy oven cleaners. Then, to make sure we couldn't be philosophic in spite of Oven-E-Z, someone else invented the glass oven door. It wasn't compulsory to keep pot bottoms bright and shiny until they developed no-rub metal cleaners and coaxed us into hanging the cooking equipment on the walls to show it off. Grandma didn't have all those handy vacuum tools for getting at hard-to-clean places, so she could forget the cranny behind the stove until spring cleaning time.

Don't let anybody kid you. Housework is just what it's always been: housework.

"Now that houses practically run themselves, women have lots of free time for creative, meaningful outside activities."

This is a trap, and we've fallen right smack into it. We *don't* have lots of free time for outside activities, meaningful or otherwise, but we're ashamed to admit it. Each of us wants to be The Woman of Today, the one we keep reading about, who's brisk, vibrant, dynamic, culturally aware, politically oriented and always on the go. That's who we want to be, and we're determined to succeed at any cost.

Ask yourself this: How often have you attended a 10 A.M. meeting, leaving the beds unmade and the dishes unwashed? How many times have you sat through a lecture on contemporary art, kicking yourself for forgetting to take the hamburger out of the freezer before you left? And as you sat there, looking at the other women around you, didn't you just *know* that every one of them had their households running like clockwork? Didn't you feel certain that you were the only woman present who didn't have a casserole ready to pop into the oven for tonight's dinner?

I thought so! Yet it never occurred to you *not* to attend the meeting, did it? On the whole, this is probably a good thing. Women *should* get away from the housework, but let's quit pretending that there isn't any housework to get away from.

Speaking of all this free time we're supposed to have nowadays, what about children? Child care is a subject largely avoided by proponents of carefree modern living.

Oh, there's some airy talk about disposable diapers and no-iron playclothes, but nobody has much to say about the children themselves. Yet children are as much a part of modern living as the pop-up toaster. Maybe more so. Certainly they play a pivotal role in contemporary life whereas, in Grandma's day they were relegated to the outer edges—the nursery, the attic and the backyard.

Even the most rabid modernists couldn't classify having the kids around all the time as a work-saver. Therefore, they must include children among Meaningful, Creative Activities. It's a debatable point.

Of course it's fun to do things with children—to take them on walks, on picnics, to plays, puppet shows and ball games. But *all the time?* Must they be in on everything from cocktail parties to watching the Late Late Show on TV?

Grandma could fix a beady eye on her offspring and order them right straight upstairs to bed this minute. In Grandma's day, Mother was always right. There were no two ways about it. Today—well, we all know what it's like today. The kids are always right. Or—if they're wrong—it's ours, their parents' fault. If Junior gets sent home from school for sticking out his tongue at the teacher, we don't blame Junior. We ask ourselves where we failed.

This may be progress, but it keeps Junior's mother pretty busy. She not only feels conscience-bound to spend long hours with Junior trying to build a better parent-child relationship, but she has to read Spock and Gesell and attend panel discussions on "Hostility in Children" and "Understanding the Pre-adolescent."

"Women never had it so good."

Oh, is that so? My grandmother found time to retire to her bed for a rest every afternoon from two to three. And that must prove *something.*

How Tame Were My Teens

My timing has been terrible from the very start. When I was born, it was no bed of roses being a baby, believe me. It was the boot-camp era of infancy, when they began toughening you to face life the minute you checked in. They didn't pick you up between feedings for fear of spoiling you. If it wasn't time to eat, they just let you lie there and cry.

By the time I became a parent, they'd adopted a new policy. Now babies were supposed to be cuddled and coddled and fed when hungry, no matter how unreasonable their clockworks might be. This made infancy pretty deluxe if you were a baby. If you were a baby's parents, it was exhausting.

But, reviewing my life, I think the rawest deal of all was my adolescence. I guess I must have *had* an adolescence, although nobody seemed aware of it. Certainly no one mentioned it. If adolescence existed when I was in my teens, it was on a very small scale. It wasn't an important social problem, like urban redevelopment and flood control. It wasn't even a proper subject for dinner table conversation because of its overtones of sex. In those days, sex was pretty hush-hush.

Now, of course, sex has replaced the weather as a handy conversational icebreaker when you don't want to bring up sensitive subjects like pop art and zoning ordinances. But back in those days, people didn't use words like "puberty," at least not without lowering their voices. And you certainly never saw anything like that printed right out in black and white on a PTA discussion-group program.

When I graduated from undershirts, my mother gave me a book called *Growing Up* and made a standing offer to answer any questions I might want to ask. That was all that happened in recognition of my advancing years.

I didn't gain status in the household. Nobody seemed to realize that I had entered a new and difficult phase of development. I'm not even sure they knew I *was* an adolescent. And it wouldn't have made much difference anyway. In that unenlightened era, becoming an adolescent didn't entitle you to the special privileges of a recognized minority group.

Adolescents then were so loosely organized that nobody paid any attention to them. Manufacturers were totally unaware of their potential as a mass market for charm brace-

lets, bulky sweaters, acne lotions, leather jackets, pop records, dual carburetors and name blouses.

The clubs we organized were small and insignificant,
pitifully lacking in power and influence. We never enjoyed
the outer-directed togetherness of being card-carrying members of the Hi-Teenettes or a nationwide fan club.

Nobody undertook vast national surveys to determine
how much time we spent talking on the phone, how late
we stayed out on dates, what percentage of us went steady
and which foods, records, movie stars and clothes we pre-
ferred.

We had no percentages or statistics to back up our
fervent pleadings, "But everybody else gets to . . ."

When we look back, our disenfranchised state seems
pathetic. We were so easy to outwit. Our parents would
discuss the bone of contention with a few of their friends
(invariably the strictest, most fuddy-duddy parents in
town) and report back to us, "Nobody else allows their
children to . . ."

We were lucky if they didn't add, "And moreover . . . ,"
taking away some privilege we already had—like staying
out till midnight. We couldn't slap a newspaper in front
of our parents' faces and crow, "See! It says right here in
the paper that 76 per cent of high school students get
to . . ."

There were no magazines directed especially to teen-
agers and their problems, among which pimples and parents seem to share top billing. We didn't know we had so
many problems, and that it was normal for us to feel miserable. Our parents didn't know it either, and they didn't
understand that we had sound physiological and psychologi-
cal reasons for being moody, sullen and uncommunicative.
They unreasonably expected us to behave nicely, no matter
how we felt.

There were no Teen Talk columns in the daily papers,

and no one to whom we could write letters signed "Be-wildered," pouring out our hearts. We were on our own— except for our parents who, of course, didn't understand us at all.

We didn't understand *them* either. Since we weren't exposed to a daily crop of letters from other adolescents registering complaints about their families, we weren't aware that all parents are unreasonable, tyrannical and hopelessly square. We were so isolated from the mainstream of life that we thought it was only our own and our friends' parents who were impossible. And there wasn't much we could do to fight back. Our parents were invincible in their conviction that they knew best.

Now that adolescence has reached its Golden Age and parenthood has been reduced to custodial service, I'm the mother of teen-age daughters.

That's my life for you. Poor timing all the way. I've never yet been a member of the ruling class. Every time I was on the verge of making it, a revolution took place and the Establishment was stripped of its power.

And there I was again, in with the underprivileged Outs. Talk about beat generations!

WHAT Begins at Forty?

My seven-year-old, Molly, was genuinely puzzled by my fortieth-birthday lamentations. "But Mommy," she said, "I thought you were *already* old!" My mother understood only too well. "How do you think *I* feel?" she asked. "I'm your *mother!*"

There is no getting around it. Forty is one of life's turning points—the start of middle age. Horrid as it is, it can't be kicked under the carpet or prettied up with talk about "the quintessence of youth." What help is quintessence when you're trying on clothes in a fitting room with a three-way mirror? Certainly it's nicer to refer to middle age as "maturity," but, like calling green beans *"haricots verts à l'Anglaise,"* the difference is academic.

As for books like *Life Begins at Forty*, and articles that take the oh-pooh-forty-is-young line, they're comforting to read, but they're about as close to the truth as near beer. You don't see any books titled *It's Fun to Be Twenty* because everyone already knows that. And who'd buy them? Twenty-year-olds are out living it up, not sitting at home reading about it.

When you get down to brass tacks, forty is forty. Take those Job Opportunity ads that say "Women over forty need not apply." Even if you had no intention of applying, it stings. Almost every cosmetic house features nourishing facial creams, specifically created for women forty and over. The Junior League disengages its members when they reach forty and, by an odd coincidence, the Young Republicans and Young Democrats use the same dividing line.

Hair rinses and hormone creams are helpful in their way, but forty is still no joke. The only thing I can say in its favor is that it beats thirty-nine—which *is* a joke. At thirty-nine you are subjected to a barrage of low humor ("You and Jack Benny, huh?") and people peer at you suspiciously as they try to figure out how old you *really* are. Thirty-nine should be skipped, like the thirteenth floor in hotels. At least when you admit to forty, no one suspects you of lying about your age.

No one suspects you of anything else either. My best friend blithely suggested that her husband take me out to dinner when my husband was out of town. And off she skipped to her Spanish class, secure in the knowledge that her husband was in safe hands.

A fortieth birthday is the moment of truth, and a rude

awakening it is. You emerge from slumber with a vague feeling of depression which you can't pin down. Then you remember. It's your birthday! Quaking with apprehension, you check to see if you've developed liver spots overnight, and relief washes over you as you realize that nothing so drastic has occurred. You look and feel about the same as you did yesterday—which isn't saying much, since you haven't worn a two-piece swimsuit for some time now, and you haven't been able to look up a telephone number without glasses for years.

But the plain fact is, you don't *feel* forty. How in the world did you get so old so young? Why, you don't even feel grown-up, much less mature. Where are the wisdom and character you'd expected to acquire by this time? What happened to the tact and sophistication you should have picked up over the years? Where, for that matter, is the nest egg you should have salted away and the portfolio of stocks you'd planned to secure? Here you are, clearly retarded for your age. Just a forty-year-old mixed-up kid.

Painfully sensitive about your own age, you become acutely conscious of everyone else's, and you discover that most people are younger than you are. This is logical enough, but it's a shock—especially when an authority figure like a school principal or a surgeon turns out to be your junior. How can you have any confidence in the diagnosis of a mere broth of a boy whose diploma, framed right there on the wall, proclaims that he graduated from medical school the year your second child started kindergarten? It's even worse when you look around you and discover that the world is being run by juveniles. After you've spent the better part of your life looking up to judges and Cabinet members as mature, dignified individuals whose age and wisdom commanded respect, it comes as a jolt to realize that Congress is full of rosy-cheeked striplings and the President is *not* old enough to be your father.

It becomes increasingly evident that you have been around for some time. All the jokes you hear sound vaguely familiar, and half the people you meet remind you of someone else you've seen before.

One of the checkers at my neighborhood supermarket looks exactly like Mrs. McMillan, who was postmistress at the beach where we spent summers when I was a child. What I mean is, the checker looks the way Mrs. McMillan looked *then*. I saw Mrs. McMillan last summer, and now *she* looks like Grandma Moses.

I may be especially prone to see resemblances, so I don't know if anyone else has my particular problem, which can best be illustrated by an incident that happened at a cocktail party. I edged cautiously into the room, gazed at a sea of strange faces and, mercifully, spotted a rumpled-haired gentleman who looked familiar. I pumped his hand and burbled, "How marvelous to see you! You're looking grand!"

He returned my greeting with a surprised expression and mumbled, "It's been a long time, hasn't it?"

I felt rebuffed and confused because he obviously hadn't the faintest idea who I was, but I still had the persistent conviction that I'd met him before. It came to me hours later—when I was home in bed. It doesn't seem likely that it could have been he, but what *is* G. Mennen Williams doing these days, anyway?

Upsetting as it is to find yourself facing it, there *is* a life after forty. What's to be done about it? What is the secret of perpetual middle age? The trick, I suspect, is to burn that bridge when you come to it. You can't just sit there, lamenting your lost youth and plucking out your gray hairs. You've got to develop a positive attitude, however little there is to be positive *about*.

To prove that my heart's in the right place, I have a couple of pieces of mildly constructive advice:

Don't pretend that you don't care how you look.

When you're a sweet young thing with roses in your cheeks, you can admit winsomely that you don't use anything on your face but plain soap and water. If you're a mere slip of a girl who looks fetching in a bikini, it's cute to confess that you're the world's worst glutton. But, at forty, ingenuousness loses its charm. If you admit that you eat like a horse, the response you'll get is a nod, meaning, "So *that* explains it."

Don't embroider your age on your bib.

I don't exactly advocate lying about it. That's every woman's own personal decision. (In my own case, it's impossible. I still live in the city where I was born, and I'm surrounded by people who can, and do, recall when I graduated from Lincoln High School.)

In any case, honesty does not compel you to reminisce about the first ninety days of the Roosevelt Administration or the time you saw Ruby Keeler in *42nd Street.*

Try to remember not to call the refrigerator the icebox or the stereo the phonograph, and try to forget that you ever heard of the NRA, Joe Penner and Ella Cinders.

Why these remnants of the misty past should remain crystal clear in my mind, I don't know. Especially since I can't remember where I put the car keys five minutes ago. But that's forty for you.

SIX

KEEPING UP GETS ME DOWN

Separate Vacations?

I'm impressionable. Easily led. When someone says, "Oh, c'mon!" I c'mon. A couple of weeks ago I was led straight down the garden path by a magazine article which airily promised that I could make a gingerbread house for my children. As a result of that fiasco, I'm going through a cautious phase.

That's why I didn't rush straight to the Pan Am office to book a ticket for the Bahamas the minute I finished reading the article recommending separate vacations for husbands and wives. Oh, I was tempted. A two-week loll on the sands at Nassau or Acapulco sounds toothsome, especially when I compare it to my usual fortnight in a rented cabin at Lost Lake with my husband, three children and a wet spaniel.

There has been a lot of alluring talk about separate vacations, and the idea makes sense. Family vacations being what they are, isn't it far more civilized for the family to disband so that each member can follow his heart's desire? Certainly a short separation from one's beloved would heighten mutual appreciation. And to top it off, the whole concept has a nice touch of jet-set sophistication. Don't the Duke and Duchess of Windsor take separate vacations? And Prince and Princess Radziwill?

It's a perfectly logical thing to do, but I keep bumping into trouble with logic. Unarguable precepts like "Live within your budget" and "Honesty is the best policy" have a nasty way of collapsing on me in the clinches. And that's why I haven't been to Pan Am yet. As I said, I'm in a look-before-I-leap mood, and I have a few questions to ask first:

What will my husband do on his separate vacation?

I suppose he could go fishing. But for two whole weeks? All by himself in the wilderness? I doubt that he'd cotton to the article's suggestion that he join a group sightseeing tour or a hiking expedition. And I'm positive he wouldn't agree to my proposal that he stay home and paint the house. So what *will* he do? I can't help remembering a remark he made last summer as we were driving to Lost Lake, and the children were squabbling in the back seat about who got to sit next to the windows. All of a sudden he turned to me and said, "You know where I wish I were going? To Las Vegas. All by myself." What kind of a heart's desire is *that* for a family man? Of course he may have been kidding. But how can I be sure?

What will our friends think of the idea?

The article warned that our friends might be slightly shocked at first, and I'm afraid that's true. We don't move with a really In group. For instance, I know only one person who's been through analysis, and I hate to think what *she'd* say if we took separate vacations. She's already convinced that I have repressed hostilities toward my husband because she once heard me complain that he kicks out the covers at the foot of the bed.

What can the children do on their separate vacations?

The article advised sending them to camp. This is an excellent idea. Camp is a wholesome and enriching experience, and I'm pretty sure the children wouldn't actually carry out their threat to run away if we sent them to camp. They'd like it, I think, once they got there. And besides, when they saw all the other children at camp, they'd realize they were mistaken in telling us that every other child in the whole world is going to either Disneyland or Europe this summer.

What about extramarital romance?

The article admitted frankly that it could happen, but it assured me that I wouldn't be interested in anything like that if my marriage is basically secure. I *think* my marriage is basically secure, but even so, I can't help wondering what I'd do if an attractive man invited me to have dinner with him. I'm afraid I'd be so taken aback I wouldn't know what to do. But the alternative of *not* being invited to dine with an attractive man is disturbing, too. There I'd be, on a moon-drenched island—surrounded by gay laughter, tinkling glasses and the strains of "Some Enchanted Evening"—dining alone with a magazine at a table for two.

Can we afford separate vacations?

The article came right out and admitted that money

might be a problem, but it discussed the subject in a calm, encouraging manner. It said that separate vacations need not necessarily be more expensive than family vacations. I suppose this is true if the family ordinarily spends vacations on safari in Africa or skiing in Austria.

Still, all is not lost. The article pointed out that financial problems can be solved with a little ingenuity. I'm not sure I know what that means. Saving money out of household budget? Selling Christmas cards door to door? Returning the empty pop bottles to the store for a refund? I don't think a little ingenuity would solve the problem in my case. Could I perhaps win a $25,000 Bake-Off contest? No. I haven't that much ingenuity.

Would separate vacations really heighten our appreciation of each other?

I suppose we do take each other for granted but, actually, I'm awfully fond of my husband, and the thought of being separated from him scares me a little. I depend on him. He tells me when I'm about to light the wrong end of a filtered cigarette, and he holds his little finger on the knot when I tie a bow, and he's amazingly adept at closing suitcases that are too full. I'm not sure I could get along without him at Nassau.

Suppose, though, that I learned to tie bows and bolt down luggage all by myself? Would it be good for our marriage if I learned that I could get along without my husband? It's a disturbing thought. But even more disturbing, do I want him to discover on his vacation that anything I can do, Room Service can do better?

Dinner at Sevenish

When a woman lies awake at 2 A.M. muttering to herself
". . . fourteen . . . sixteen . . . eighteen . . . twenty . . ."
she could be counting sheep and she could be counting
her blessings, but it's a lot more likely that she's counting
the people whom she absolutely must have to dinner. Almost any woman can click off a list of social debts that out-
numbers her supply of dessert forks by a ratio of at least
three to one.

"Oh dear, we owe everybody we know!" is a cry of

despair from the heart. The question is, what to do about it?

The most tempting solution is to pay off—that is, entertain—everyone in one swoop at a great big party. It's a lovely thought, but impossible. Where would all those people sit down? Even if they don't sit down, the house isn't big enough. And besides, you can't afford a party like that.

The alternative is a series of small dinner parties, but where in the world do you *start?* Armed with paper and pencil, you dash off a list of four couples for your first dinner. A nice congenial group it is, and you can seat eight comfortably at your dining table. But wait a minute! You've forgotten something—namely, yourself and your husband. *Now* what? You can squeeze yourselves in, and crowd ten people around the table or you can eliminate one couple and go to all the trouble of polishing silver and fixing *coq au vin* just to pay back three couples. On the other hand, you can forget about the dining table and have a bigger party— say, twelve or fourteen. People will have to eat off their laps, of course, and your husband considers that barbaric.

At this point a woman is likely to make the mistake of consulting her husband for advice, and a crucial mistake it is. Men simply do not understand the basic philosophy of entertaining. They cling to the childish notion that having a party is a simple matter of asking some people over and giving them something to eat. They haven't even a rudimentary grasp of the complexities and nuances involved. Ask a man for suggestions on whom to invite, and he'll rattle off the names of your best friends—the only people in the world to whom you *aren't* indebted.

Ask him for menu suggestions and he'll list his own favorites: cold meat and potato salad (impossible because it's too simple); pot roast and potato pancakes (impossible because it's too difficult); spareribs and sauerkraut (simply impossible).

If you remind him that your guests fed you on squab and wild rice, he can't see what difference that makes. Neither can he understand what you're making such a fuss about. If a party is all that much trouble, his advice is to skip it. Forget the whole thing. He can't believe that any woman but you would get herself so worked up just because she's having a few people to dinner.

Wretchedly, you suspect that he may be right. You wonder if other women do get into such a swivet about entertaining. Their parties seem so relaxed and effortless. Maybe their silver is always polished, their coat hangers straight, their bathrooms immaculate and their vases filled with fresh flowers. Maybe they even mean it when they say, "Oh, I didn't fuss at all. It's just a simple little supper." You say the same thing yourself, of course, but you can't imagine anyone taking you seriously. How could you produce veal blanquette and almond torte without fussing?

Still, you must play by the rules, so you telephone your invitations in the proper offhand manner: "Can you join us for a bite of supper on the twenty-second? Very informal. Around sevenish."

From that moment on, you will spend a lot of nights lying wide awake, mumbling, ". . . eight . . . ten . . . twelve . . . fourteen . . ." You're figuring how many dessert plates you'll have to borrow from your mother; counting the number of rolls you'll have to buy; estimating how much meat your guests will eat; totaling the mushrooms you'll have to stuff.

The party looms in your mind as a stage production in which your house, your furniture, your cooking, your tableware and that awful worn spot in the hall carpet will be exposed to public view. This, in turn, leads to nightmares in which your guests arrive to find you stark naked with your hair in curlers, your house a shambles and nothing whatever to eat.

There will be many times during the days ahead when you will find it necessary to hold your breath and count to ten very s-l-o-w-ly to keep from screaming:

At your next-door neighbor, who borrowed your party-size coffeepot and didn't return it, and is now lapping up the sun at Puerto Vallarta for two weeks.

At yourself for taking all those useless college courses in Romantic Poetry when you might have been learning something really worthwhile—like the art of flower arranging.

At your middle daughter, who tells you on the morning of the party that she forgot to tell you that Mrs. Partridge called a couple of days ago to say that they wouldn't be able to come because they were expecting some very dear friends from out of town, and of course they wouldn't expect you to include two extra guests.

At the cat, who staggers into the house with a torn ear while you are setting the table and has to be taken to the vet.

At the cheery voice on the telephone, which rings just as you are unmolding the chocolate mousse, to inform you that Rumpelmeister's is having a special, this-week-only sale on percale sheets.

At your husband, who spends the ghastly half hour before the guests arrive sitting on your carefully plumped cushions, dirtying three ashtrays and saying, "Why don't you just relax?"

But finally the guests do arrive. And at this point—no, not quite at this point because one party is pretty much like another in the early stages when people are being introduced and the ladies are sizing up each other's dresses, but, say, within half an hour after the guests arrive—comes the moment of truth when the tone of the evening is set.

If fortune smiles, the party will shift gears, pick up momentum and *go*. The guests, who barely five minutes earlier were standing around discussing the late spring or the early frost like strangers waiting for a bus, are now—well, take a look at them. Hank Anderson, over there by the window, has Julie Callahan and Tim Byers convulsed with laughter over his story about the psychiatrist and the stripteaser. The Leonards and the Boydens are chatting animatedly, having made the happy discovery that they had the same guide in Mexico City. Lucy Macdonald is listening, enthralled, to Bill Ames's interpretation of Edward Albee's latest play, and Maggie Ames and Letitia McAdoo are sitting on the love seat, waving their hands and whispering about the Copleys' divorce. The party has burst into life and become a *party*.

Cynics ascribe this phenomenon to the relaxing effect of the cocktails, which have had time to numb the higher brain centers and reduce inhibitions. I mention this theory because if I don't, someone else will, but I don't believe in it. I've been to parties where the martinis were just as potent, just as plentiful and just as quickly downed, and the guests spent the *whole evening* acting like people waiting at a bus stop. So why do some parties come alive, pow! while others just lie there, limp and droopy?

Experts like Perle Mesta and Amy Vanderbilt insist that advance planning is the keynote to success. They stress careful attention to details: a pretty table, festive food, plenty of ashtrays and, above all, a congenial, well-balanced guest list. This advice reads nicely but parties, like parenthood, can be planned only up to a point. From that point on, what happens is anybody's guess.

Take that advice about the guest list, for example. It's simple enough to sit down with paper and pencil and work out, according to mathematical formula, a pleasant blend of doctors, lawyers, merchants and chiefs; a proper proportion of pretty women and witty women; and a workable ratio of introverts to extroverts. No, I take that back. It isn't simple. It's just about impossible, and what makes it so is convention's decree that both members of a married couple must be invited. In order to ask Charlie, who's such an asset at a party, you've got to include Henrietta, who sits there like a sphinx and doesn't contribute a thing.

But let's say, for the sake of argument, that you've surmounted all obstacles and come up with a perfect guest list. Or better yet, let's say *I* have. There was a time, about a year ago, when I thought I'd done exactly that.

An old friend who works for the State Department in Washington wrote that he'd be out our way and available for dinner on the fourteenth. Naturally we wanted to have a party for Pete, so I took pencil in hand to make out a guest list. Since Peter was an ebullient extrovert, I needn't rack my brains for life-of-the-party types. He could handle that department all by himself. Bill and Sue Armstrong seemed a good choice because Bill was running for the state senate, and would be eager to hear the political scoop from Washington. And Sue is charming and very pretty.

"Wait till you meet Pete!" I told them. "He's a character. Knows more insidey political dope than Drew Pearson."

I said the same thing to Marge and Dexter Bennett. I asked them because Dexter is a conservative stockbroker, and I envisioned him having a spirited ideological debate with Ken Forbish, an artist and a way-out liberal, whom I'd also invited. Then, too, Marge Bennett has a wonderful sense of humor, and I knew she'd appreciate Pete. "He does a marvelous imitation of General de Gaulle," I told her. "It'll knock you out."

I added the Winfields because they'd just returned from Sun Valley, which gave them something in common with the Springers, whom I asked because they're nice and I'd owed them for ages. And there I was, with a perfectly balanced party of twelve. Or so it seemed at the time.

The party didn't turn out the way I'd planned it. Pete was the big disappointment. Our guests eyed him with puzzled little frowns and I ran around whispering, "I just can't understand it. He seems so—well, uh, different."

Different was no word for Pete's behavior. He stood in a corner by himself, smiling vaguely and cracking his knuckles. Except for commenting three times on how much our children had grown, he didn't have anything to say. When I tried to draw him out by asking what was new in Washington, he shrugged and answered, "Oh, not much. Just the same old things happening to different people."

He acted like a butterfly who'd reverted back to the caterpillar stage, and I couldn't figure it out. Had he had a lobotomy? Were he and Mary getting a divorce? As I found out later, in a letter he wrote apologizing for his lack of vivacity, the explanation was far less bizarre. He was simply coming down with a cold.

Pete's torpor threw the whole evening out of whack because I'd counted on him to provide most of the conversation and the other guests to serve as appreciative listeners. As it was, the good listeners had to talk to each other, and that didn't work out very well.

Dexter and Ken talked to each other, all right, but their conversation wasn't a lively ideological exchange of views. They sat off in a corner, reminiscing about a mutual friend in Cincinnati whom nobody else had ever heard of. The Winfields and the Springers never got around to comparing notes on Sun Valley because Joe Winfield and Cliff Springer discovered another and far more engrossing bond. They had both recently given up smoking, and they spent practically the whole evening swapping withdrawal symptoms. Bill Armstrong got a telephone call from his campaign manager and spent over an hour talking on the phone, so his evening wasn't totally wasted. The ladies sat on the sofa, discussing the problem of finding a good cleaning woman until Sue Armstrong, who is normally the soul of tact, changed the subject by asking Marge Bennett when her baby was due. Marge had to admit that the baby was two months old and, at that point, everyone began looking at their watches and muttering that tomorrow was another day.

That was one party that wasn't. As I dejectedly emptied ashtrays and turned off lamps, I asked myself what Perle Mesta would have done in my place. Should I have passed around sheets of paper and asked the guests to see how many words they could make out of "Constantinople"? Should I have rolled back the rugs and cried, "Let's dance"?

I honestly don't think so. Even supposing that I were a born leader (and I'm not), those guests of mine, an uncooperative bunch if I ever saw one, weren't about to get pushed into any new activity that might prolong an already interminable evening. True, it wasn't the guests' fault that the party was a flop. They weren't aware of the roles I'd assigned to them, so they could hardly be blamed for not playing them. I'd counted on their acting true to type, which people often don't for a multitude of reasons ranging from a bad day at the office to blues in the night. Or, as in Pete's case, a stuffy nose.

Which is not to say that it's pointless to scratch your head over a guest list, or that you may as well adopt a let-the-chips-fall-where-they-may attitude. Drawing names out of a hat isn't the answer. Sure, we can all recall terrific parties where the guests were a wildly assorted hodgepodge of ages, politics, clothes and types. Still, I'm inclined to believe that those crazy, mixed-up parties are less terrific at the time than they are later, in retrospect, when you can look back on them as enlightening experiences and tell hilarious stories about the weird characters you met the other night. At the party itself you're apt to wonder uneasily why you were expected to hit it off with those kooks.

The fact is that birds of a feather do at least speak the same language (although those old familiar phrases tend to make one party sound like a taped recording of another). But strange breeds must contend with a language barrier that may prove insurmountable. If you have ever found yourself the sole writer at a gathering of merchandise managers (or a merchandise manager surrounded by avant-garde artists) you know what it is to "wander lonely as a cloud."

A friend of mine ran into this dilemma when she found herself at a party where all the other women seemed to be up to their eyebrows in the symphony ball, the art museum benefit, the League of Women Voters or the Junior League thrift shop. My friend said that people kept opening conversations with her by asking, "What do you do?" So she finally told them, "I have six children. *That's* what I do."

Party food is another area fraught with hazards. Certainly, it ought to be a bit special. When the ladies are wearing their lowest necklines and the gentlemen have shaved twice in one day for the occasion, it is hardly befitting to serve them hot dogs and baked beans on paper plates; and even roast beef and browned potatoes, while undeniably good, does seem a bit uninspired. Still, it's possible to veer too far in the ultra-ultra direction. Lobster thermidor and butter curls may so overawe the guests, if they're not accustomed to that sort of thing, that they'll talk only in whispers. But this doesn't happen often, the price of lobster being what it is. It's more likely that a hostess will get carried away by her new gourmet cookbook and serve something overly imaginative. Veal with tuna-fish sauce will impress the cognoscenti no end. They know that it's *vitello tonnato*, which was featured in *Vogue* and is very chic. But to the uninitiated, it seems a pretty funny combination, and they may speculate that something must have gone terribly wrong out in the kitchen.

It's worth mentioning, too, that culinary disasters—if handled with finesse—can absolutely *make* a party. This is a comforting thought to keep in mind when you're trying out that new recipe for fish timbales, with which you intend to impress that snooty Loretta Sewell who served you duck *à l'orange*.

I treasure among my memories one party in particular, at which the *pièce de résistance* was chicken divan, a *haute cuisine* dish consisting of creamed chicken poured over broccoli stalks and served in individual casseroles, topped with grated cheese. When the hostess brought it on, it was greeted with gasps of admiration because it did indeed look beautiful. But, as one guest after another tried to put a fork into it, consternation appeared on their faces. The broccoli, which had been put into the casseroles frozen, on the optimistic assumption that it would emerge bubbling hot from the oven, was still frozen solid. The hostess, acting with enviable aplomb, made no apologies. She simply shrugged, shooed the guests back to the living room for another drink and sent her husband out for Chinese food. The guests, giddy with relief at being spared the ordeal of convincing a trembly-lipped hostess that broccoli encased in ice was *delicious,* spent the remainder of the evening confessing their own most embarrassing experiences to each other, and it turned out to be one of the gayest and most convivial parties ever.

Naturally, I wouldn't advise planning a culinary catastrophe to make a party a sure-fire success. In truth, there *is* no way to guarantee success. A good party depends on such a complex and unpredictable set of circumstances that it seems to just happen. Or maybe it doesn't. A party is a sometime thing.

Speaking for myself, when I lie awake at 2 A.M. mumbling, ". . . fourteen . . . sixteen . . . eighteen . . . twenty . . ." I find it helpful to recall what the gambler said as he placed his last two dollars on the roulette wheel: You can't lose them all.

Merry Avalanche

Exchanging Christmas cards is a wonderful way to keep in touch with auld acquaintances, half of whom you wouldn't recognize if they fainted in your arms. In my own case, the proportion of unknowns is probably nearer 75 per cent. Our Christmas card list includes 400 names. Who *are* these people anyway? Obviously, we don't have 400 friends. Nobody has 400 friends. To put it in a nutshell (and a better place for it would be hard to find) they are simply the names on our Christmas card list. The list is scribbled on the back of an old laundry sheet, but every one of those names is as permanently inscribed as if it were carved in granite.

A few years ago, when my husband and I still had illusions, we tried to cut down our Christmas card list. We struck off the names of good friends whom we saw all the time. We could extend greetings to them in person. We lopped off all the unidentifiable names. We agreed that it was silly to send cards to my cousin's mother-in-law, whom we'd met once, and to the dentist in Guadalajara who fixed a broken filling for my husband six years ago. Chances were, these people racked their brains trying to recall who *we* were when our cards arrived. Needless to say, we learned our lesson. All these auld acquaintances had our names on their lists and, as their cards poured in, we felt more and more Scroogelike and ashamed of ourselves. Three days before Christmas, I rushed downtown to buy extra cards and we stayed up until 3 A.M. addressing them.

Now our custom is to order fifty more cards each year than we sent last year. Death, alone, erases a name from our list, and we scour our brains for new names to add. We send cards to people simply because they live on our busline. After all, we tell ourselves, Christmas comes but once a year. At this rate, we'll be sending 1,000 cards in 1976. But with the world situation what it is, I'm not going to worry about *that*.

Anyway, Christmas-cardwise, I have a number of other problems to occupy my mind:

Choosing the card. I spend November picking out our Christmas card. What I mean is, that's just about *all* I do in November. I give up nonessentials like plucking my eyebrows and defrosting the refrigerator. Last year, in a misguided attempt at efficiency, I took the advice of a stationer who sent me word in late September that the holidays were just around the corner. He urged me to drop in soon, before the rush, and make my selection while stocks were complete. I dropped in bright and early the next morning, and the result was that I spent October and November picking out our Christmas card.

I'm nobody's fool, and I don't make a mistake like that twice. This year I didn't even think about Christmas cards until the day after Halloween. Barely four nerve-wracking weeks later, I arrived at a decision. In case you're on our list, you may wonder why—after examining every Christmas card in the world—I chose a mouse dressed in a Santa Claus suit, hauling a Yule log. By what mental process did I reject thousands of other cards and select that mouse to convey our holiday greetings?

Actually, it's a bit difficult to explain and my husband never *will* understand. He prefers to regard that card as just another piece of evidence that I am irrational.

"Why," he keeps asking, "why can't you ever choose a decent Christmas card? Why do ours always have to be so damned cute?" (His idea of a really terrific card is one that says "Season's Greetings" and has a black-and-white etching of a pine bough laced with snow.)

My moment of decision occurred quite suddenly on a late November afternoon. I was, as usual, sitting at the Christmas card racks, plowing doggedly through album after album of cards. I had just pushed one book aside and reached down to hoist another hefty volume from the floor to the counter. And suddenly I went limp. I couldn't, I simply couldn't, go on like this. Mental collapse was just around the bend, and the point of no return was RIGHT NOW! The sight of one more chubby angel, another glimpse of a tipsy Santa waving a martini glass might, at this point, unhinge my fragile grip on sanity. I had to stop searching for the one perfect card and settle on something, *anything,* or I'd be spending the holidays in a nursing home under deep sedation.

I sat up straight, blinked my eyes to clear my head and took several deep, steadying breaths. That's when I saw it. There, in a book open on the counter, was the mouse.

Hailing a clerk, I placed my order for 400 mice.

Preparing the cards for mailing. It's good policy to keep a telephone book handy to check addresses on the list for possible errors. And it's a nice idea to write personal messages on the cards, such as "Long time no see" or "Our best love to you all." But I'm afraid that I put these little niceties into the same category as peeling tomatoes—a good idea to keep in mind for next time.

Of course, I *do* have to stuff, seal, stamp and address every single one of those envelopes. It's a simple task. Any twelve-year-old child could do it. Does anyone know a twelve-year-old child who's not busy?

Arrival of incoming cards. I react to the arrival of our first Christmas card with the same emotion that I feel at the first twinge of labor pains. It's a blend of excitement and panic. In both cases, I realize that it was bound to happen, but I certainly didn't expect it *now*.

Naturally, I had intended to have our own cards ready for mailing by this time. But when the postman delivers the first card, ours are still in their boxes, untouched since they arrived from the store.

The first card not only makes me realize that the hour groweth late. It brings home to me, with dismaying clarity, that our own card is a dud. The first card is always a little gem. That's why it was sent early. So it would get the attention it deserves. It's either terribly expensive or very original. The originals are the most upsetting. After all, it isn't my fault that I'm not rich. But it *is* my fault that I'm not creative and can't make stunning, abstract linoleum prints. Why don't *I* get any captivating ideas, like taking a picture of my children standing on the roof, patting a stuffed reindeer? Why didn't it occur to me to write a witty, newsy chronicle of our family activities during the past year?

As a matter of fact, it *did* occur to me, but I couldn't think of much to report. We had the kitchen painted, and Molly learned to ride a two-wheel bike, and we finally managed to housebreak the dog. And, oh yes, my husband gave up smoking. But our family accomplishments seem paltry compared to the dazzling triumphs catalogued in those jolly mimeographed bulletins. Indeed, I become quite depressed about the even tenor of our days as I read:

"Well, it's been an eventful year for the Hollingsworth family. Not too much peace and quiet, but more than our fair share of fun and excitement. Joe senior was named vice-president of the company in April. Answering his three telephones and dictating letters to his two secretaries proved so enervating that he bought a boat to 'get away from it all.' Now he spends weekends serving as president of the Yacht Club and piloting a twin-engined 36-footer over the bounding main, and he has to go to the office to relax. Seriously, our boat, which is named 'Small-4-Chin' (get it?), is great fun, and we're becoming accomplished sailors. You should hear us talk nautical!

"Young Joey is in the fifth grade, and pitcher on a Little League team which won six games out of eight this season! We're proud to report that he won first prize in the school science fair for a chart he made on the dietary habits of white rats.

"Susie, who is now a VIP eighth grader, enjoys her piano lessons as much as ever, and her teacher tells us that she shows real promise. Susie is in the Gifted Child Program at school and, to our amazement, she is currently reading 'War and Peace.' But it isn't all work and no play for our

Susie. She's the champion skate-boarder of the neighborhood!

"Mommy read 'The Feminine Mystique' which convinced her that it wasn't enough to be 'just a housewife.' So she became a schoolgirl. On June 8, she got her MA in psychology, and on June 12, Melinda Anne, our caboose baby, was born—all 6 pounds, 7½ ounces of her. She is a blue-eyed, curly-haired blonde who wins the hearts of one and all.

"Not to be outdone, Bijou, our silver poodle, gave birth to a litter of five puppies four days later!"

You see? Even their *pets* are high-achievers!

Puzzling cards. Every year we get a pretty card from Bert and Alma with a handwritten message that always says the same thing: "We think of you often and we'd love to see you. A happy Christmas to you all, Bert and Alma."

We feel exactly the same way about *them.* We think of Bert and Alma often and we'd love to see them because then maybe we'd remember who they *are.* We send them a card each year, too, which is easy because the return address is clearly written on the envelope, postmarked Des Moines. The thing is, we can't recall knowing anybody who lives in Des Moines. Still, the way people move around these days, that proves nothing.

My husband's theory is that Alma is the sweet-faced lady who ran over our dog seven years ago. It was Skeezix's fault for running in front of her car, and the lady was very nice and helpful and drove him straight to the vet's, where he subsequently made a complete recovery. My husband keeps asking me, "Don't you remember?" I *do* remember, very clearly. But I'm almost positive that lady wasn't named Alma. I think her name was Mary Biggs. Or maybe Barnes.

My theory is that Alma used to be the waitress at the pizza parlor at the lake where we go summers, and Bert was the cook. Or maybe Bert was the manager of the apartment house where we lived right after we were married, and Alma was his wife. I don't suppose we'll ever know for sure, and it really doesn't matter. Alma and Bert sound like lovely people, and I've grown quite fond of them over the years.

What disturbs me more are those handwritten notes, penned in illegible scrawls. We get several of them each year, and we try hard to decipher them because it's just possible that someone might be trying to tell us something we ought to know. But scrawls aren't as undecipherable as that tiny, cramped handwriting that looks like seismograph recordings of earthquakes. And worst of all is that free-flowing penmanship that looks like ocean waves drawn by a four-year-old, in which *m*'s, *u*'s, *w*'s, *v*'s and *r*'s are all exactly alike. Still, as I say, we try.

"This letter from Nancy or Mary somebody-or-other," says my husband. "Why does she say she's sorry to hear my lips are chapped?"

"What?" I ask.

"It says here," says my husband, "'I'm sorry to hear that Jim's lips are chapped.' Why would anyone write us a thing like that? Besides, my lips *aren't* chapped."

"Let me see the letter," I say. "Where does it say that?"

He points, and I read where he points. "Why, it doesn't say that at all!" I tell him. "It says she's married—no, worried. She's worried for fear the pigs have flipped. Or maybe it's tripped. And," I add, reading further, "she's sending us chipmunk cheese."

"Use your head!" says my husband. "She sends Christmas cheer. *You* ought to be able to figure that out. You wished everyone a wevy wenny Chutvus yourself."

Displaying the cards. I used to display as many cards as possible on the mantel over the fireplace. Others I arranged tastefully on tables and shelves, and I tucked a few into picture frames. The rest I dumped into a large wooden salad bowl which I put on the coffee table. This custom had one real advantage. It was impossible to dust the living room. It also had one real disadvantage. Drop-in guests always eyed the display of cards in search of their own. When they didn't find it (it was always buried in the salad bowl) they looked hurt and I felt embarrassed. Now I toss all the cards into the salad bowl and put holly on the mantel.

What to do with the cards after Christmas. You can't just dump Christmas cards into the garbage can. It seems so cold-blooded. Some people, I'm told, paste them into scrapbooks and send them to hospitals and convalescent homes. This is a kind and thoughtful thing to do. Still, it bothers me. Do shut-ins really enjoy looking at someone else's old Christmas cards during the January white sales? If so—if they're *that* desperate for diversion—it's a national disgrace and Congress should look into the situation.

Actually, old Christmas cards aren't much of a problem in my life. I have an eight-year-old who catches lots of colds, and she likes to cut out. On nasty winter afternoons, when television palls, I'm *glad* we exchange Christmas cards with 400 people.

SEVEN

SOME GOOD, SANE, PRACTICAL, DOWN-TO-EARTH ADVICE FROM A NONEXPERT

How to Help Your Husband Understand His Wife

The incomprehensibility of women is a myth invented by men. Pretty smart of them, too. It frees them from the obligation of trying to figure out their wives.

When confronted by what he considers inexplicable behavior, the average husband shrugs his shoulders and mutters, "Women!" thus implying that it is futile to ponder the irrational ways of the feminine sex. Such an attitude is not only defeatist, but just plain ridiculous. Women aren't all that hard to understand, and any man who is willing to put forth a little effort (surely no more than he devotes to his tax loopholes) can learn to get along more or less serenely with his wife.

Because I am keenly interested in helping my own husband understand his wife (and assuming that other women have similar aspirations) I have composed a list of things a man should never, *never*, NEVER say during moments of stress when a wife is particularly prone to feel mismated and misunderstood:

"Honey, do try to look at this problem in perspective."

To the masculine mind, this doubtless seems a marvelously sensible piece of advice, based on the sound philosophic premise that all things are relative. And it's undeniably true that a cigarette burn in the new sofa *isn't* the most cataclysmic event that ever occurred. Viewed in relation to the Peloponnesian Wars, the situation in Southeast Asia and the current flu epidemic, it pales into insignificance. Nonetheless, a husband had better think long and carefully before dishing out this particular kernel of wisdom. A man who went into a three-day funk over a putt he missed in a tournament is in a weak position to philosophize about the triviality of minor mishaps in the total scheme of things.

"It looks fine to me."

When a woman vouchsafes that her old tweed coat is irrevocably out of style, her husband should accept her opinion as fact. Nothing is to be gained by arguing the point. In the mystique of fashion, a man should recognize his limitations and confine his criticism to telling his wife when her slip shows. He should no more presume to offer advice than his wife should attempt to tell him which dry fly she'd prefer if she were a trout.

True, there are exceptions. I've heard wild tales about husbands who actually enjoy shopping with their wives.

Still, it's a rare man who has the expertise to tell a raglan sleeve from an accordion pleat, and husbands should be cautioned not to speak up in defense of the old tweed coat.

In this situation, a man has only two alternatives. If he can afford it, he should tell his wife to buy a new coat. If he can't afford it, he should tell her he *wishes* she could get a new coat.

Either way is almost certain to win him a smile and perhaps a kiss.

"Why don't you sit down for a few minutes and relax?"

She is having eight people to dinner, the cleaning lady failed to show up, the table still isn't set and the cucumber-and-pineapple ring didn't jell. This is not the moment for a man to tell his wife to sit down and relax. This is not the moment to tell her that he adores her. He shouldn't even ask if there's anything he can do to help—unless he really *can*, which is unlikely. At a moment like this, a husband should simply GET OUT OF THE KITCHEN!

"Can't we discuss this calmly?"

When a lady is stamping her foot and screaming at her husband, it behooves him to yell back and call *her* names so that she can burst into tears and accuse him of not loving her any more. After a really satisfying scene like that, she'll be more than willing to kiss and make up. But if he persists in the folly of being calm and self-controlled, she'll think he *really* doesn't love her. And then goodness only knows what might happen.

"Will you promise not to get mad if I make a suggestion?"

Would the Russians agree to negotiate under such conditions? For that matter, would *we?*

When a woman moans that she's absolutely exhausted and her feet are killing her, she wants sympathy. She does not want a dissertation on the irrationality of wearing high-heeled, square-toed shoes. If a man feels that he *must* get his opinion off his chest, he had best come out with it. His wife will be hurt, angry and resentful. But if he makes her promise in advance not to get mad, she'll be *furious*. Personally, I wouldn't blame her if she threw something at him.

Parenthetically, I'll admit that women often use this same underhanded device by making their husbands promise not to catch cold, and later saying, "See? I *told* you not to go duck hunting on such a wet, blustery day!"

Still, nothing is to be gained at this point by bringing up *her* faults, and I probably shouldn't have mentioned it.

"Darling, you look fine. Nobody will notice your . . ."

There is no situation in which a man should tell a woman that nobody will notice her. If the copper rinse she used has turned her hair bright orange, she'll know he's lying. If the case in point is merely a run in her stocking, she'll interpret his remark to mean that her legs aren't worth looking at.

"Dear, would it cheer you up to go to an Italian place for dinner and then a movie?"

Taken at face value, this seems a kind and considerate suggestion. But if you look deeper (as a wife in a dejected frame of mind is sure to do) it turns into an insult. What does her husband take her for, anyway? A frivolous flibbertigibbet whose emotions are so shallow that she can switch moods just like *that?*

She has just discovered her first gray hairs, and she is sunk in deep, soulful contemplation of youth's flight and time's wingèd chariot hurrying near. She isn't about to snap out of her doldrums and clap her hands in glee at a chance to go out to dinner. Would Antigone have shrugged off her problems if somebody had invited her to the movies? Would

Hamlet have attemped to lift Ophelia's spirits by offering her spaghetti and meatballs?

Then, too, a wife might harbor the suspicion that her husband suggested going out because he doesn't relish the thought of an evening at home with her. Come to think of it, why did he specifically mention an Italian place? *He's* the one who's so fond of minestrone.

"You're making a mountain out of a molehill."

The molehill at issue is Junior's report card, and Junior's mother is terribly upset about it. Junior's father, in taking an optimistic, boys-will-be-boys attitude, is playing his cards all wrong. *Someone* in the family has to show concern over the boy's grades and, if his father won't, it's up to his mother.

If Father really wants to calm Mother down, he should go completely to pieces. Rave and tear his hair. Make it clear that he's worried sick about the boy's lack of initiative. Mother will brighten up immediately, and assure Father that Junior is a fine, upstanding lad with a brilliant mind. He's just a little slow in getting started. Like Winston Churchill.

"Let me bring you a sleeping tablet so you can quit worrying about it and get some sleep."

This would appear to be a sound, practical suggestion, considering that it is 1 A.M. and she is sitting bolt upright in bed with the light on, chewing a pencil and muttering to herself. She has to conduct tomorrow night's PTA meeting and introduce the guest speaker, and she doesn't know what to say or how to say it.

But let's take a closer look at that sound, practical suggestion. On analysis, doesn't it really mean that her husband wants her to take a sleeping pill so that *he* can get some sleep?

Should she fail to cotton to this idea (and she will)

the cooperative husband will not take the easy way out by gulping down a Nembutol himself. Instead, he will welcome this opportunity to win her respect and admiration by writing her speech and explaining Roberts' *Rules of Order* so that she can understand them.

Then they can both go to sleep with a clear conscience.

"Please tell me why you're so upset!"

When a man has no idea why his wife is sitting there sighing and twisting her hankie, he should put his arms around her and murmur, "There, there, honey, I understand," and sooner or later, he will.

Maybe she's worried about getting fat. Maybe she's depressed over the world situation. Maybe she's not sure, herself, why she feels doleful. Life being what it is, it's some times hard to pin these things down.

Yet she expects her husband to understand her. If he were a sensitive, perceptive person he'd be attuned to her moods, and he'd know why she's troubled. If he *doesn't* know, he's an obtuse, indifferent egocentric who pays no attention to her.

Therefore, a man should never, *never* ask his wife why she is melancholy. If he has to ask, he'll get the answer he deserves:

HE is the reason why she's so upset.

The Magazine Women Sneer At

Since we do not subscribe to *Playboy* (my husband reads it at the barbershop, which may explain why he gets so many haircuts) my knowledge of the magazine was limited. Oh, I had seen it, of course. I'd picked up a copy now and then off the drugstore magazine rack, and glanced at the photos of Playmates and Bunnies. But until the morning I discovered a whole pile of *Playboys* under Katie's bed, I had never read a man's magazine for content.

I was amazed. It wasn't the playmates that shocked me.

I'd seen them before, and it was no surprise to find the young ladies as butterfingered as ever at holding their bathtowels. Actually, I suppose those triple-page, fold-out, suitable-for-framing photographs should have prepared me for the *Playboy* philosophy. But I was taken aback by *Playboy*'s frivolous attitude toward life, love and marriage.

In my innocence, I had taken for granted that the how-to article in women's magazines would be matched by constructive advice in magazines for men. I had envisioned articles along such lines as "How to Bolster Your Wife's Ego," "How to Fix a Broken Roller Skate" and "Treat Your Wife to Sunday Breakfast in Bed."

Men's magazines *do* publish how-to articles, but they're not the sort that contribute much to domestic harmony: "How to Win at Poker"; "How to Cure a Hangover"; "Where to Stay in Las Vegas"; "How to Mix a Dry, Dry, Dry Martini"; "How to Succeed with Women" (which has nothing at all to do with getting along with one's wife).

Neither are there any articles in *Playboy* on the career and/or marriage theme, so dear to the hearts of women's magazine editors. Apparently it has occurred to no one to ponder whether a *man* can combine marriage and a career, although it strikes me as a legitimate question. Can a man truly fulfill his role as a husband and father when he flies out of the house at 8:10 A.M. and arrives home, tired and preoccupied, after the children are bathed and ready for bed?

Men's magazines differ radically from women's in their attitudes toward sex. Women's magazines approach sex as a problem, rather like calculus, which can be mastered only by diligent effort, earnest application and vast patience. Men's magazines take a less complicated view. Sex is sex, and the more the merrier.

While women's magazines are conscientiously examining marriage from all angles and knocking themselves out to promote emotional maturity, higher housekeeping standards, balanced budgets, self-improvement and mutually satisfying conjugal relations, *Playboy* (operating on the assumption that its readers are unmarried or wish they were) concentrates on examining Elke Sommer in the nude from all angles.

Is this fair? I ask you. Why should women be continually admonished to slipcover that chair, curb those extravagances, change that hairdo, firm those sagging muscles, stuff those peppers, shampoo that rug and stop that pouting, while men are egged on to live it up and enjoy themselves? It goes without saying (but I refuse to leave it unsaid) that it *isn't* fair. Something ought to be done to mitigate the discrepancy between men's and women's magazines.

It happens that I've given this problem a good deal of thought (it occupied my full attention while I was sitting under the hair dryer this morning) and it seems to me that the best solution is a new entirely different type of women's magazine. No, not *Playgirl*. I don't believe the feminine market would go for that sort of thing. What I have in mind is a revolutionary concept in women's magazine philosophy, a fresh new attitude toward its readers. Instead of urging women to ever greater heights of accomplishment and self-improvement, this magazine will sooth its subscribers with assurances that they are perfectly wonderful just as they are. Maybe even *too* perfect.

The new periodical, which will be called *Bad Housekeeping* (The Magazine Women Sneer At), will print no articles of the how-to-polish-your-silver-to-a-professional-luster type. Its leitmotiv will be the how-not-to point of view, exemplified by such titles as: "Dine by Candlelight and Eliminate Silver Polishing!" "What's So Bad About an Uneven Hemline?" "Nobody Loves a Perfect Hostess!" "Who Looks Under Your Beds, Anyway?" "Carrot Curls Are a Crime Against Nature!"

Bad Housekeeping's human interest stories will not be inspiring accounts of faith and courage overcoming great obstacles. We will never recount the triumphs of a mother of eight who delivers her own babies, bakes her own bread, holds down a full-time modeling job in addition to her paper route and, in her spare time, weaves rugs and studies for her law degree. Our articles will focus on phlegmatic types to whom our readers can feel superior: "Confessions of a TV Addict"; "I Have a Super-electronic Range, But I'm Still a Lousy Cook"; "She Stays in Bed till Noon While Her Children Run Wild"; "How I Parlayed $100,000 into 75 Cents in My Spare Time."

We'll print no pictures of contemporary dream houses with custom-designed kitchens to make our subscribers swoon with envy. On the contrary, we'll encourage them to count their blessings and appreciate their own primitive living conditions. Our magazine will be illustrated with pictures of dingy, inconvenient kitchens, cramped closets and sagging porches. Every bed photographed in *Bad Housekeeping* will be unmade, and all electric appliances will predate World War II.

Our cooking department will include a monthly feature called "The Worst I Ever Tasted," illustrated with photographs of weepy meringues, curdled sauces, soggy cakes and watery stews. Our recipes will assuage our readers' guilt feelings about feeding their families wienies twice in one week. At least they aren't serving *our* suggestions for curried parsnips and liver loaf with beet sauce.

Our table of contents will include a regular feature titled "The Most Uninteresting Person I Ever Met" to make our readers feel cheerier about the lack of colorful personalities in their own lives. Sample titles: "My Insurance Broker's Political Opinions"; "Weather Predictions of My Next Door Neighbor"; "Down Memory Lane with an Auto Mechanic."

Our medical department will be handled with prudence

and restraint to avoid scaring our readers out of their wits. Instead of printing case histories documenting pathological symptoms in vivid, clinical detail, we'll insert a blank page, headed, "Don't Tell Me, Doctor, I Don't Want to Know."

Our beauty section will give our readers a much-needed boost in morale by featuring photographs of women so dowdily gowned and unbecomingly coiffed that anyone would feel glamorous by comparison.

Our diet pages will hail no new miracle diets, guaranteed to take off four pounds of excess weight a week. *Bad Housekeeping* will take a bold, unprecedented step and tell its readers the truth: that *all* diets are miraculous, the miracle being that anyone could live on 1,000 nasty little fat-free calories a day. To help women accept their current poundage with equanimity, we'll run an article titled "Who Wants to Be a Size Ten, Anyway?" postulating the theory that skinny women are mean, wicked and maladjusted, and pointing as examples to Lady Macbeth, Salome and Empress Wu Chao. (For all I know, these villainesses may have been built like tubs, but I don't think that matters. It's the *spirit* of truth that counts.) To bolster our thesis that plumpness is pretty, we'll illustrate our diet section with portraits by Rubens and Renoir, whose models ran from size 18 to 20½.

Our garden department, espousing defeatism as its editorial policy, will publish a think piece titled "Throw In the Trowel!" which will begin: "Inasmuch as several thousand varieties of thrips, mites, weevils, worms, aphides, midges and beetles are pattering around in your flower beds and licking their chops, it behooves you to act sensibly and admit you're licked. Successful gardening is impossible unless one has the round-the-clock zeal and selfless dedication of a Buddhist monk, which is not a desirable goal for a well-balanced woman. . . ."

The article will go on to point out (1) that the difference

between weeds and flowers is a state of mind, and (2) that moles give a garden that lived-in look. This should lift the spirits and lighten the consciences of our subscribers, who might otherwise feel they should be scrounging around the herbaceous borders on their hands and knees instead of lying in the hammock, reading *Bad Housekeeping*.

And there it is—a rough prospectus for our first few issues. If *Bad Housekeeping* strikes you as a brilliant inspiration and the perfect answer to the harried, hounded, guilt-driven housewife's need for solace, you are a woman after my own heart. If you disagree, if you can't understand how any normal, intelligent American woman could possibly be interested in such a silly, useless, flighty magazine, it's a safe bet you're a man. And probably a *Playboy* subscriber at that.

Love in a Nutshell

Do you need romantic advice? Are you puzzled? Bewildered? Perplexed? Bring me your little problems. Don't be embarrassed. There is no problem so simple that it doesn't confuse me, too. Okay. Let's take your questions one at a time.

Q. How can I be sure of marrying the right man?
A. Bless your heart, dear, you can't. Marrying a man is like having your hair cut short. You won't know whether it suits you until it's too late to change your mind.

Q. Don't you think it's terrible the way some people marry perfect strangers?

A. There's nothing wrong with marrying perfect strangers. It's *im*perfect strangers that cause such nasty shocks.

Q. What qualities do you consider important in a marriage partner?

A. Strength of character, good looks, a sense of humor, a pleasant disposition, an attractive personality, financial security, good family background, intelligence, sensitivity and emotional stability.

Q. Gee, I don't know anyone like that.

A. Me either.

Q. Then you think a girl should settle for less than her ideal man?

A. Ask yourself this: If you did find an ideal man, would he marry *you*?

Q. My boy friend says he fell in love with me at first sight, but he can't analyze his reasons. Can you?

A. Not exactly, but I suppose they're similar to his reasons for ordering sirloin tips on the businessman's lunch. It just happened to appeal to him.

Q. But he proposed to me the first night we met, without knowing anything about me. I can't understand that.

A. Neither can I, but males are baffling creatures. A man will spend months of research before deciding which car to buy, but he'll select the mother of his children without even kicking the tires, so to speak.

Q. What do you mean by *that*?

A. Not what I think you think I mean. All I'm saying is that a man should at least find out the name, age and cereal preference of the woman with whom he'll be eating breakfast for the next fifty years or so.

Q. I am a twenty-year-old girl with a 36-23-36 figure, and my hair is naturally blond. My problem is that these three boys want to marry me, and I don't know which to choose. Bruce is tall and good-looking and a wonderful dancer, but can't seem to hold a job. Ken has gobs of money and a white MG, but he's two inches shorter than I am. Rupert's the one my mother wants me to marry because he's older and established in business, but our horoscopes conflict. He's Scorpio and I'm Gemini. Which boy should I marry?

A. If I were you, I wouldn't marry any boy who'd marry a girl as silly as you.

Q. If two people enjoy doing the same things, isn't that a good foundation for marriage?

A. What things? Dancing divinely together? Walking barefoot in the rain? Sharing a passion for pepperoni pizza? None of these activities will occupy much of your time when you're married. Now, if you can paint a garage divinely together or work out a budget in perfect unison, you might have the makings of a harmonious marriage.

Q. But don't you think it's important to marry someone with whom you have interests in common?

A. Not especially. Once you're married, you'll have plenty of interests in common. The bank statement, the morning paper, the leftover pot roast in the refrigerator, a joint income-tax return and a landlord who thinks you use too much electricity.

Q. Where does love fit into the picture?

A. Everywhere. Anywhere. It is the quintessential ingredient that makes marriage work. But what *is* it? It's trickier to isolate than the virus that causes the common cold.

Q. Isn't there some way to tell real love from infatuation?

A. Someone (probably George Bernard Shaw—it usually was) said that you should ask yourself what you'd think of your beloved if you were both the same sex. I doubt if that's the definitive answer to your question, but it's a point worth pondering.

Q. I am a twenty-three-year-old girl and, frankly, I'm worried. I've never met anyone I want to marry. How can some girls marry such impossible men?

A. Men are the only other sex there is.

Q. Am I correct in assuming that you believe in long courtships?

A. Why no! What gave you that idea?

Q. You did. You said that people should know something about each other before they get married.

A. Did I say that? Well, I take it back. I haven't any opinion on the subject. I know a couple who rushed off to a justice of the peace the moment they discovered they both got goose pimples when they heard Ella Fitzgerald sing "I've Got You Under My Skin." They'd known each other scarcely six hours. Last week they celebrated their fifteenth wedding anniversary, and they still hold hands at the movies. I know another couple who went together four years before getting married. They were ideally suited in every way. Even their *mothers* liked each other. Yet barely a month after the honeymoon, they were consulting a marriage counselor.

Q. Don't you think it's romantic to be a young man's first love?

A. Yes, but it's a lot better to be his last love.

Q. But if he marries you, can't you take that for granted?

A. Not exactly. I'd say the wisest procedure is to treat marriage the way you'd handle an unbreakable record. Trust that it's every bit as durable as it was guaranteed to be, but don't drop it on the floor to make sure it really *is*. To belabor the point, even a *fragile* record can last a lifetime—if you take good care of it.

Q. I am a seventeen-year-old girl who's madly in love with a boy eighteen. Our parents think we're too young and financially insolvent to get married. I don't think money is important if two people love each other. Don't you agree?

A. Yes and no. Money isn't important as long as you have enough of it.

Q. How much is enough?

A. That's hard to say. Another woman's model kitchen can make you feel awfully poor.

Q. Do you think it's possible to reform a man?

A. All things are possible. The odds are about equal to your chances of finding a pearl in an oyster.

Q. I'm getting married soon, and I'm worried that I don't know everything I ought to know. Can you recommend a good sex manual?

A. I'm afraid not. Sex manuals upset me. Actually, *all* books that contain instructions of the Step 8 (see Diagram 8) type make me nervous. The two most helpful books in marriage are a good cookbook and a balanced checkbook.

Q. But don't you agree that sex information helps people to cast off their inhibitions and get more enjoyment from the act of love?

A. We-ell, yes. Up to a point. But too much technical information can be as repressing as Victorian prudery. When you're concentrating on the program notes, you can't hear the music. Enjoyment of sex depends—as most things do—on attitude. And that's what is so depressing about those marriage manuals. Their earnest approach to sexual fulfillment brings to mind *The Little Engine That Could*. I doubt that grit and determination are the keys to success in this particular sphere. Spontaneity, enthusiasm, tenderness and a spirit of adventure are better virtues to cultivate.

Q. Whatever happened to sentimental love? People aren't as romantic as they used to be.

A. People never *were* as romantic as they used to be.

If Romeo and Juliet had lived to celebrate their first anniversary, they'd have had their differences, too.

Q. Isn't that the truth? Marriage isn't all moonbeams and roses. It's an emotionally sustaining partnership between two people who are able to resolve their hostilities and compromise their differences through mutual respect and understanding. Don't you agree?

A. No, I don't. And if I did, I wouldn't admit it. That's the kind of talk that takes all the sparkle and fizz out of marriage. Can you imagine Marcello Mastroianni saying a thing like that?

Q. You keep contradicting yourself. I don't believe you know what you're talking about.

A. I'm talking about love—the most illogical, perplexing, mystifying subject in the world. How can I be expected to apply reason and logic to something that's as capricious and unpredictable as next year's hemlines?

Q. But what are you driving at? What's your point? You don't make sense.

A. *Naturally* I don't make sense. That's my point, in a nutshell. That love is the most paradoxical, confusing, incomprehensible, indefinable—

Q. Oh, don't start that again! Surely you must have something constructive to say on the subject. What, in your opinion, is an ideal marriage? Answer me that.

A. I'll be glad to. An ideal marriage is when—I mean, it's one in which two people love, cherish and manage to put up with each other through all the difficulties, crises, annoyances and complications caused by their marriage.

Advice from a Left-Handed-Mitten Collector

Are you one of those brisk, decisive individuals who can toss out a deck of cards that's absolutely perfect except that the eight of clubs is missing? Can you dispose of a left-handed mitten that's been kicking around the closet all winter?

No? Me either. If you're like me, you keep every wire coat hanger that finds its way into your house because who can say when two or three hundred coat hangers mightn't come in handy?

If you're like me, you ought to be ashamed of yourself. Come on, let's put our addled heads together and try to figure out what to do with all that stuff we've been collecting through the years. By talking some sense into you, I might persuade myself to get rid of those negatives I've been saving just in case I should want an extra print of my high school graduation picture or that snapshot of Old Faithful.

What should you do with that old sewing machine in the garage that you intend, any day now, to paint white, decorate with Pennsylvania Dutch decals and plant with ivy?

You know what you should do with it? Give it to a rummage sale. Yes, yes, I'm aware that you *bought* it at a rummage sale because you heard another woman say that she'd like to paint it white and turn it into a conversation piece for her front hall. She wouldn't have done a thing with that sewing machine either, and the fact that you bought it right out from under her nose is just her good luck.

What should you do with those stacks of old magazines that contain interesting articles you plan to read just as soon as you find a little spare time?

There are two kinds of articles. There are those (like "The Secret Liz Never Told Richard" and "Are You Headed for a Nervous Breakdown?") that demand to be read, hot off the press, the moment the magazine arrives; and there are those (like "Our Water Resource Problem" and "How to Remove Spots and Stains") that you certainly plan to read, but not right now. You want to wait until you have time to concentrate properly.

I won't say that the day will never come when you'll be ready to read that article on water resources. But if it should—if you awaken some morning with a yearning, burning desire to get your hands on that article—you needn't rummage around in your basement, getting cobwebs in your hair and breaking your fingernails. All you have to do is go to the public library and tell the librarian what you want. She'll find that article for you in a jiffy. I've no idea how she tracks it down so fast, because the library must have an even larger collection of old publications than you and I have. But that's her problem, not ours.

Now get rid of those stacks of paper in your basement. I think the Boy Scouts collect old newspapers and magazines. They do something constructive with them. I believe they turn them back into trees.

What should you do with those twelve jars of bread-and-butter pickles that Aunt Bessie sent all the way from St. Louis, and that you aren't especially eager to open because they look sort of peculiar?

Aunt Bessie, bless her heart, put them up with her own two hands, and they took nine whole days to make. She said so in that cute note she enclosed with the pickles. Aunt Bessie is a sweetheart and you're crazy about her.

But look at it this way: she'll never find out that you dumped those pickles into the garbage can. On the other hand, suppose you *do* open them and they explode, causing serious injury to you and your household? If Aunt Bessie found out that her pickles were responsible for a dreadful accident like that, she'd never forgive herself.

Now go right downstairs, throw away those pickles and write Aunt Bessie a nice note telling her how much you're enjoying them.

What should you do with that blue and white polka dot dress that's in perfect condition, just as good as the day you bought it seven years ago, and that's bound to come back into style sooner or later?

Come now, put on your thinking cap! You *know* why that

dress is still in mint condition. Because you never wore it, that's why. The minute you got that dress home from the store you noticed something that you'd failed to perceive while the saleslady was rhapsodizing about its imported fabric and unusual shade of blue, which brought out the color of your eyes. That dress—there were no two ways about it—made you look thick through the hips.

Since you're a good five pounds heavier today, it's unrealistic to expect that polka dot number to be more flattering now. As for its coming back into style, that's about as likely as the Navy going back to schooners. Look, honey, when the fashion magazines speak of "recapturing the mood of the Thirties," you mustn't interpret it as a go-ahead to drag out the beaded chemise your mother bought for her trousseau. The fashion industry couldn't permit you to do such a thing. After all, Bill Blass and Tina Leser have to make a living just like the rest of us.

So get rid of that dress. By the way, have you any idea where it is? Could it be in that box in the attic marked "Sprg. Thgs, 8/16/59"? No? Well, maybe it's in the bundle labeled "Slps, Jns & Sks."

If you do manage to find it, for goodness' sake don't succumb to the temptation to tear it up for dustcloths. The fabric's too slick for dusting, and you already have enough dustcloths to supply the Hilton hotels.

What should you do with that jar of pinkeye ointment that you've been saving because you might want to renew the prescription one of these days?

Are you absolutely positive that salve is supposed to cure pinkeye and not athlete's foot? All the label says is "Use four times daily as directed."

Anyway, medical science has made tremendous advances in recent years, and that label is dated 4/9/56. Surely, during the past decade they've made some progress in the treatment of pinkeye.

While you're tossing out that jar, get rid of the other junk in your medicine cabinet. All those empty tubes and those bottles with purple sludge at the bottom.

What should you do with the baby furniture that's been gathering dust in the basement, but you're afraid to give it away because everyone knows that the surest way to get pregnant is to give away the baby things?

That's the silliest superstition I ever heard! There are lots of young families that could use that crib, and it's ridiculous to hang on to it because of an old wives' tale. . . . On second thought (unless you'd like a little wee one to cuddle) perhaps you'd better hang onto it after all. I'd hate to feel responsible for giving you reckless advice and—well, you never know. Besides, you'll have grandchildren someday, and that buggy and crib will come in handy.